# Kevin Gould's

# loving and cooking

## with reckless abandon

Quadrille

First published in 2002 by
Quadrille Publishing Limited,
Alhambra House,
27-31 Charing Cross Road,
London WC2H OLS

Text and photography © Kevin Gould 2002
Design & layout © Quadrille Publishing Ltd 2002

Creative Director: Mary Evans
Editor & Project Manager: Lewis Esson
Design: Françoise Dietrich
Assistant Editor: Katie Ginn
Photography: Kevin Gould
Home Economist: Jane Suthering, Angela
Boggiano and Jane Milton
Production: Tracy Hart

Grace

All life is one
and everything that lives is holy:
Plants, animals and people
All must eat to live
and to nourishing one another.
We bless the lives
that have died to give us food.
Let us eat consciously,
Resolving by our work to pay
the debt of our existence.

*John G Bennett*

Cataloguing in Publication Data: a catalogue record for this
book is available from the British Library

ISBN 1 903845 53
Printed and bound by Kyodo Printing Co., Singapore

This book is about you, not me. It recognizes that a recipe simply distills experience, and can only be a copy of a collection of processes the true memory of which lie elsewhere. I hope, though, that these stories and recipes inspire some new memories in you, and that you will now accept the recipes as your own. Like an alchemist's formula, a recipe cannot of itself include the special sensitivities required of the cook - it takes Love to transform your subtle energies into truly nourishing food.

Before we enter further into the spirit of loving and abandonment, the fourteenth-century Sufi mystic Rumi should remind us that bashfulness is a barrier, and that we must abandon our timidity: 'Cut the throat of shame!' he pleads. His manifesto is for passion, pure and simple:

'Reason is powerless in the expression of Love.
Only Love can reveal the secret of Love.
If you want to live, be in Love.
Be in Love to stay alive!'

I was astounded to receive, via email, His Holiness the Dalai Lama's injunctions for living well in the 21st century. Astounded, not because the spiritual leader to millions of Tibetan Buddhists was suggesting moral guidelines by which to live right, but because of the last tenet: 'Approach Love and Cooking with Reckless Abandon'. The other tenets were, as you might expect, laudable and wholly worthy, but the idea of recklessly letting go, of being brave enough to surrender to the unknown, proved so irresistible that it ignited the flame of abandon in me. The fire of that flame has sustained me as the book has been written, and will, I suspect, burn here forever. I hope that you, too, will be warmed by its light.

Friends – it is time to come out of the kitchen cupboard: loving and cooking with reckless abandon!

With Love,

*Kevin*

Kevin, realfood@dishy.net
London, January 2002

(You should know that I contacted HH's office to ask for permission to use the title, but his Religious Assistant explained that this was not a quote from the Dalai Lama, but had been disseminated by a 'well wisher'. My thanks to you, whoever you are.)

# chapter one
## farmers, fishermen and their produce

Your cooking is an expression of you. Just like your handwriting or your dress sense, it helps to explain how you see yourself, and to describe who you are. And just as you might choose a certain pen to write with or favour threads from a certain designer, so you can bring those same sensibilities to bear on your food. While building a framework for loving and cooking with reckless abandon is our final aim, we must first start with ingredients, the construction materials that are going to lay the foundations for this great work.

'Conventional' farming is a relatively recent invention. Until the late 1800s nearly all farms were mixed (operating a system described even unto the Bible), which required crops to be rotated, thus refertilizing the soil, and land left fallow one year in seven. Crops do not only take nutrients from the ground, they also replenish it, hence a mixed-crop rotating system feeds and re-energizes the soil. In addition, by allowing the land periodic rest, bacterial, insect and animal life proliferates, due initially to the nitrogen-rich grasses that thrive on fallow ground, making excellent feeding for livestock, whose hooves churn the topsoil, and whose dung fertilizes the land. Result – a simple, virtuous system.

Russian Mennonite (Anabaptist) pioneer settlers in the American Midwest had been raised on a mixed system in their homeland, although they had been, for the most part, tenant farmers, effectively working the land on behalf of its owner, who would take as rent a percentage of the crops grown. The freedom they must have felt on seeing those huge American spaces allowed them the chance, for the first time in their lives, to think beyond the back-breaking serfdom of small-field mixed farming. The Midwest needed a suitable crop to populate its plains, and the Turkey Red wheat that the Mennonites brought with them from Russia was the answer. A heavy cropper, with twice-yearly harvests, Turkey Red was enthusiastically planted across the Midwest prairies, in fields the size of counties. Up until this point, wheat bread was a nob's refined luxury; most early Americans derived their carbohydrates from coarse rye breads and potatoes.

As wheat became more available, economies of scale in production meant low prices, and the USA's love affair with wheat blossomed. Cheap wheat meant bread and cake for all. Less positively, prairie-sized fields needed artificial fertilizer to compensate for lack of natural nutrients they'd have benefited from in a mixed system. Depleted earth cannot be fully re-energized by artificial means, with the result that, by the 1970s, soil over vast tracts of the American Midwest was, by all technical yardsticks, sterile.

Sterile earth contains no food for worms, whose oxygenating and nitrogen-fixing activities in the soil must be replaced in part by chemical application. No worms means no food for birds, whose absence in turn allows a host of other winged pests to invade the crops, requiring more pesticides. The lack of biodiversity created by monoculture, with its attendant chemical intervention, therefore causes water reserves to be poisoned, as artificial fertilizers, herbicides and pesticides seep into aquifers. The spectre raised is of diseased crops, chemically treated, then fed with tainted water. (And they called it progress!) Mass monoculture, intended and expected to be a money-saving exercise, ends up being expensive, with short- and long-term cost implications.

All of this is good news for the chemical companies, whose sales ever multiply, but bad news for the crops, in which measurable traces of the dread chemicals survive. These have a definite effect on the quality of the crops harvested, and in turn on your body. Most crops are sold by weight, making nitrogen-based fertilizers the mass-grower's friend, as crops fed on these take up more (dirty) water. This may be part of the reason why organically grown crops often have more flavour than their conventional cousins – no nitrates means less water content in the food, therefore less dilution of nutrients and sugars. But more about organic after we consider genetic modification.

Make no mistake, GM foods have been with us since humans first grew crops. Farmers have always sought to cross-breed crops to achieve more useful, healthier, heavier-harvesting strains. Wheat itself is a marriage of two strains of wild grass, einkorn and emmer. About 2,000 years before the Greeks and Romans adopted this wheat in favour of their own coarse grains, the native Anatolians at Çatal Hüyük had cross-bred soft einkorn with hardier emmer, resulting in a crop that could be ground into a pliable flour, but the ears of which would not blow away on the wind-swept steppes.

Cross-breeding is an essential part of crop cultivation, and every food we eat has been the subject (and, usually, beneficiary) of it. However, like junkies in a poppy field, scientists are gorging themselves on the possibilities inherent in altering the DNA of plant life. Their minds are (as the junkies' would be) so intoxicated with the desperation for results that, often, thought is not given to the broader picture, or to any altruistic impetus that might have given birth to the research in the first place: you may start out trying to feed the 'developing world', but end up by simply patenting vitamin A-enhanced 'golden rice'. (In this particular case, the modifying of rice to 'golden' was heralded as the end to vitamin-A-deficiency-related eyesight diseases in Far Eastern people. Stock markets rose and paper fortunes were made before it was realized that said Asians would have to eat their own weight of this rice weekly if levels of beta-carotene were to increase enough.)

My feeling is that many of the scientists engaged in food-centred DNA-based research are making the same mistakes that 19th-century man made – in believing that nature is subservient to man, whose intelligence allows him to believe that he can better it. The question is whether 'intelligence' is understood as being knowledge or wisdom. Most scientific types are happy to rationalize intelligence as knowledge: information that is digested subject to the laws of logic and according to one's experience. In a world of ever-increasing specialization, where enormous emphasis is placed on training and learned behaviour, such knowledge is fashionable and is often called wisdom. To me, wisdom is the portion of intelligence that cannot be learned: in part experience, to be sure, but informed by a deeper, more subtle understanding that exists in all of us.

Back to GM... The danger is not simply in cross-breeding foods – we've agreed that this happened forever– but in scientists mixing DNA of species without heeding potential side effects. The best-known example is the tomato with the fish gene inserted to stop it from softening on the supermarket shelf. Let's face it, a tomato needs a flounder gene like a fish needs a bicycle! There is a real danger of pure strains of DNA becoming so contaminated by cross-breeding that their code will be lost. This is rationalized as an excuse to indulge in developing ever-more pernicious fungicides, herbicides and pesticides to fight the new species of predator that prey on gene-altered crops.

GM foods are intended as a way to feed people cheaply. But is organic food the answer to feeding people effectively? Hailed as the saviour for those ever more distrustful of farming practices, organic food is now a multinational agri-business in danger of falling into the same trap. Organic farming and food manufacturing are worth more than $8 billion worldwide, and now count such supra-national corporations as General Foods among their players. Let's look on this as a positive: huge, well-funded organizations have the ability to invest in organic farming practices that will make better food more widely, and more cheaply, available. Good news, you might say, apart from the fact that they are applying conventional farming and manufacturing practice to the organic market.

This means that, say, (properly certified) organic milk can be produced from cows that may eat only organic feed but live their lives on 200-acre feed-lots that contain not one blade of grass. That the milk may then be ultra-heat-treated, to allow it to be trucked across the country and stored for weeks, seems to run counter to the spirit of organic food. If the milk really were more nutritious and delicious in the first place, aren't those nutrients and fine farmy flavours killed in the heat processing? Does this mean that what we're buying is effectively expensive window-dressing – feel-good products that pander to our paranoia while compounding the problem that we had hoped they'd solve?

Perhaps this is the moment to raise the issue of food miles. No matter the purity of the food we buy, or for that matter its price, the indicator that we should be looking at is the distance it travels to get to market. Sending fresh prawns to Europe from Indian seafood farms uses fuel for every mile they must travel. One should question the economics and ethics of such projects: apart from the air pollution factor, and the fact that prawn farming ruins mangrove swamps and guarantees filthy seas, does the customer have an inalienable right to buy prawns at all times, whatever the environmental cost?

This is no anti-big-business invective. We need corporations with muscle to be behind the better-food movement so it becomes the mainstream. But if they can consider, say, organic wheat to be a satisfactory investment only if it's grown as a single crop, prairie-style, not learning from previous mistakes, we must conclude that not only intelligence, but intellect is in corporate short supply. We need to decide what organic food means to us. Some corporations believe that if customers have weaknesses for junk food, then that should also be available in organic forms. This marketing-led approach pushes products in the same way car companies offer the same tired old models in shiny new colourways.

Part of the solution, I think, is for consumers to learn to discern between good and bad organic foods. If an organic carrot is limp, it means nothing that it was grown by nuns and watered with Evian. And if a scan through the ingredients of an organic ready-meal reveals hydrogenated oil, then it matters little whether the oil was from organic sunflowers in the first place. So rather than being sold on the label 'organic', let's look Beyond Organic.

Beyond Organic is about connection. It assumes an intelligent customer who is satisfied only with the very best. Beyond Organic encompasses such down-to-earth concepts as quality, seasonality and localness, and is not sold on the strength of its packaging. The concept requires that consumers have a more meaningful relationship with the very food that sustains them; this positive flows from a negative – finding themselves cynical of product claims, merchandising devices and marketing spin, the customer simply votes with the basket, and chooses only that which can be trusted.

I'm not suggesting an Arcadian ideal whereby we would all grow our own food and weave our own clothes, but simply that we can bring less of the intellect, and more intelligence to bear on the ingredients we buy. Beyond Organic assumes that there's a part of food that cannot be measured – if you like, its energy quotient. Going Beyond suggests that any ingredient has a value beyond the sum of its amino acids, vitamins and minerals, and thus the ability to nourish the spirit, as well as the body.

Which brings us to Loving and Cooking with Reckless Abandon. You can be reckless with ingredients that are carefully grown and consciously chosen! As in those team-building exercises when you let yourself fall, to be caught in the arms of your friends, abandon in the kitchen can only happen if you trust your ingredients. Only in this spirit can the ingredients do their real work: sustaining the system and the soul. As long as there is mistrust, there will be fear. Many sages have said that there are only two human emotions – Fear and Love, and that all else is to be found in the spectrum

between. If there is fear – of contaminated food, for instance – then there's less room for love. Love is beyond organic – as Sophia Loren once said: 'The most indispensable ingredient of all good home cooking: love for those you are cooking for!'

# butter sesame carrots with fizzy water

The spa town of Vichy lies near the River Loire in France's richly fertile Bourbonnais region. To the south, and a little east, sits proud Lyons, home to France's most sumptuous, fat-enriched, calorie-laden cooking. Food lovers flock there for its famous *haute cuisine* restaurants – Paul Bocuse and Les Frères Troisgros among so many others. It is one of the few places in the world where your taxi driver from the station will recite the *menu gourmand* of your chosen destination with all the wistful longing of a teenage David Cassidy fan singing 'Could It Be Forever?'

Those same food lovers are also to be found in Vichy, where, during penitential weeks, spleens and livers are rested and bowels exercised with a regime that includes drinking copious amounts of the excellent (naturally) carbonated water that bubbles up in the Grand Pavillon and subsisting on a light diet. While the idea of eating vegetables for their own sake, rather than as an embellishment for meat or fish, may be *outré* for these epicureans, Vichy spa cuisine has given us some beautiful dishes, and has lent its name to *carottes Vichy*.

For a *carotte*, or any other vegetable, to be called Vichy, it must be cooked with butter and sugar in Vichy water, the end result being shiny and glazed. This recipe takes another look at the method, but reduces the sugar and adds some sesame seeds, bringing out the sweetly succulent character of the carrots. To enjoy this dish, you need neither an overloaded digestion nor any particular love of carrots – the fun is as much in the cooking method as in the taste.

serves 4

**preparation about 40 minutes**

1 tablespoon sesame seeds
500g middle-aged carrots
Vichy water (of course, you could use any fizzy water, but... wouldn't it be somehow nicer to square the recipe circle by honouring the place that gave birth to the dish?)
a knob of good butter

♥ In a dry frying pan, toast the sesame seeds over a gentle heat until they snap, crackle and pop, and turn Tahitian-brown. Remove from the heat and put the seeds in a bowl to allow them to cool and crisp up.

♥ Thinly peel or scrape the carrots and then slice them at an angle.

♥ Place them in a saucepan and barely cover with Vichy water.

♥ Add the butter, a pinch of salt and the sugar, and bring to a steady boil. Shaking the pan the whole time, increase the heat and marvel as the water is absorbed and evaporated.

♥ When there is only a small amount of liquid left in the pan, throw in the toasted sesame seeds and shake well to coat all the carrots.

**sea salt**
**a pinch of granulated sugar**
**some finely chopped parsley or**
**(preferably) coriander, to garnish**

♥ Serve immediately, with a sprinkling of the chopped green herb and a glass of celebratory Vichy water.

This dish marries well with Onion-smothered Chicken with Sharp Lemon and Hamine Eggs (page 82), and Porcini-stuffed Poussins (page 167).

# Florellia's caldo de papas

In Colombia, a country that venerates the potato, Florellia de Peña makes the best potato soup ever. Her son, Oscar, makes the second-best version. Oscar is 'first a Colombian, then a designer', which must make him one heck of a Colombian, because he's a truly wonderful designer. As Creative Director of Philips Design, he spends his days finding ways to make our homes more enjoyable, and more practical spaces in which to live. At home himself, and in homage to Mum, he excels with this simple soup.

'We were always happy when Mum made this *caldo*,' he explains. 'We were seven kids – and 63 cousins! – and soup stretches. *Caldo de papas* made us happy, because, as it was easy to make, it was helping Mum, too – it meant that, even though she had help, Mum would not be tied to the kitchen that night.'

At home in Bucaramanga, Oscar remembers his Grandma peeling *papas* for *caldo* 'like a machine' and is convinced that good taste at table comes from happy memories, just as flavour comes 'from engaging with food'. 'I'm very keen on food,' he says. 'The whole process – cooking is not just preparation, it's talking to the people that made or who sell the ingredients. Flavour comes from asking their advice, from being actively engaged with them. That way, the meal starts to taste good before you even start to cook!'

## serves 4

**preparation 35–40 minutes**

a knob of butter
1 large shallot, finely chopped
garlic (the amount according to whether you have a meeting or a tryst later on or the next day, but, say, 2 fat cloves), crushed to a wet pulp with the flat of a knife
sea salt and freshly ground black pepper
4 medium potatoes, sliced
olive oil
4 eggs
a bunch of fresh coriander, roughly chopped

♥ Make a *sofrito*: melt the butter in a large saucepan, then add the shallot and the garlic with salt and pepper to taste. Cook until it sizzles, then add 8 cups of water

♥ When the water boils, rain in the potatoes and a slick of olive oil.

♥ Make the potatoes comfortable in the lightly boiling water over 15-20 minutes by squeezing them a little with the back of a spoon from time to time, to encourage them to disintegrate. Remember, though, that the potatoes should have a future! They should not disintegrate completely, or be allowed to wear the respectable French clothes of a vichysoisse, but should retain their identity!

♥ When the soup is nearly ready, break in the eggs one by one. Your intention is to lightly poach them in the soup, which you should do by covering the pan and letting them cook for 1 minute.

♥ Serve immediately, an egg per person and a heap of coriander in each bowl. Remember to toast the health of Florellia Peña!

*Caldo de papas* is a great family dish, upgradeable by the addition of fried chicken, or even seafood, and is a perfect simple pleasure in itself.

He should know: having started with a single hairdressing salon in Minneapolis, Horst has now sold his company, trousering over $300 million worth of energy in the process.

But money does not buy taste, and expensive foods are not guaranteed to have more flavour than simple ones. Money's biggest problem is that it buys expectations. All our sages have suggested that, while it is fine to have hopes, expectations should be avoided. 'By God,' said Rumi, the fourteenth-century Sufi mystic, 'there is no death worse than expectation.' Many have taken this to mean that we should cast away all materialism and become wandering dervishes or the like. Let's believe, however, that Rumi's is not an injunction to be poor, but serves only as a reminder that we should respect the natural laws of transaction, and place intention and positive energy before us at every step.

If we are to avoid the empty death that Rumi warns about, then the words of seventh-century Sufi sage Ali Ibn Abu Talib are worth remembering: 'Asceticism is not that you should not own anything, but that nothing should own you.' This is not to say that there is anything inherently wrong in wanting good things, or with purchasing expensive food, and, anyway, food lovers that I know insist that they do not buy costly delicacies, but merely rent them until they eat them. Consider, if you will, that if our Creator wanted us to be poor, why give us foie gras and truffles to aspire to? Or cashmere, which, to a moth, is as good as foie gras?

As anybody who has ever felt let down by a purchase will attest, money plays a part in the transaction of energy but is not its sole element. The next time you give your money a treat and take it out for a food shopping trip, please consider that all it does is to buy you entrée into the world of ingredients, which is a very different thing from getting enjoyment from them. The other elements in any transaction include you, your attitude to your purchases and the relationships that you manage to make with those who are selling your food to you.

Oscar Peña, whose Mum's Caldo de Papas appears on page 16, says that his mind starts to taste her delicious soup whenever he buys his potatoes, coriander and eggs. More than that, he says that the finished soup's flavour depends as much on the quality of the transaction that purchased the ingredients as on the technique that makes the soup. Oscar believes that the quality of care with which the foods have been looked after, the quality of art in the foods' display and the quality of contact that he has with the person serving him all add to (or subtract from) the energetic value of the dish. As anybody who shops and cooks for somebody they truly love will agree, by willing the food to nourish their love, so it becomes nutritious and delicious.

This positive attitude to shopping for food appears to be at variance with the hard-nosed, profit-driven, disconnected world of the supermarket. For their convenience, but not ours, many supermarkets have cut down on the human element in their businesses, and mechanized their offer wherever possible. 'Convenience' and 'self-service' mean, in effect, reducing the meaningful transactions in a store to a money (OK, energy) exchange at the checkout.

The notion that we can be better serviced by serving ourselves works only for those who attach no importance to the energetic value of the food, or those who abhor social contact. Reducing the food we buy to commodity level, to a collection of pre-weighed, calorie-counted, cryovac-wrapped units, helps neither our enjoyment of food nor our ability to be nourished by it. And while I'm on the subject, 'convenience food' is designed mostly to be convenient for its manufacturers and retailers, who admire it for its chemically supported keeping properties. Don't get me wrong, though. We need supermarkets, and they need us. Let's hope we can (in the words of ex-Harvard psychology professor Baba Ram Das) come together in love, and not just in the name of convenience.

In spite of the convenient armchair possibilities promised by Internet retailing, I prefer to do the bulk of my shopping in physical stores, by way of building a relationship with my food (even with the likelihood of witnessing ugly scenes at the '8 items or less' checkout). The hunter-gatherer instinct, coupled with the potential for human contact, simply seems more satisfying than the disconnection offered by the virtual world. Which leads me to a mail order/expectation shopping story: a man buys the Charles Atlas body-building correspondence course, then writes them the following letter: 'Sirs, I have followed this course for the last three weeks. Now please send me the muscles.'

The French used to have a term for the act of food shopping. 'La petite bataille' was used to denote the skirmish that takes place between shopper and shopkeeper, each of whom is determined to get the best deal for themselves, and each of whom also recognizes that fighting a battle is not the same as winning a war. However, the tensions caused by the apparent conflicts in 'la petite bataille' have a positive, not a destructive, effect. Even though one or other party might feign frustration or anger (as a battle tactic!), the overall strategy of coming together in the name of good food serves to stimulate the appetite, and to maintain high quality and fair prices.

If you'll allow me, a tangential thought on the nature of stimulation occurred to me while watching a waiter in a smart restaurant take an order: fascinating insights are to be had on the lovemaking culture of a nation by watching how they shop for food, either in the store or at table. The French require protracted foreplay – observe the stern-faced diners' barely perceptible squirms of anticipation as, in commanding fashion, the waiter annunciates the delights of a dish, listing the ingredients, lingering over the cooking technique, tantalizing with the description of the garnish. Diners then relax into allowing as much time as is needed for the act of eating to reach its unhurried climax. The French are, by the way, acutely aware of that which constitutes 'correcte', and are accordingly uncomfortable with all unorthodox approaches.

Italians, while delighting in the same foreplay, warm themselves up by prodding the waiter, probing him for more information as to the suitability of the chef's background and intention. To an Italian diner, it is essential first to impress on the waiter his or her own culinary ability ('Chef makes it how? No! I would make it like this!'), then to allow shameless flattery to coax them into tasting a dish. Any pretence of coyness is abandoned when said plate eventually arrives, as the diners fall upon it, acceding with abandon to the pleasures of the palate. Italians talk beautifully, persuasively and at length about food, but eat very quickly.

The English start things off in a brisker, more businesslike fashion, hands held still above the table, with little movement above or below the waist. The waiter is listened to with an urbane air of detached amusement, the diners having already made up their minds as to what they'll eat. So sure are they of themselves that the English are willing to accept any wine recommendation unquestioningly, as if by doing so they are testing the sommelier rather than revealing any lack of interest in or knowledge of wine. Food for the English is required to be inventive, served piping hot, and in legendary quantities. (Guess where I'm from!)

For a lesson in negotiation, observe the Americans. No matter how rare the ingredients, how talented the chef or how perfect the menu, the waiter must offer his diners the chance to customize their meal, all the while guiding them to a satisfactory conclusion and a big tip. All tastes are catered for, and none denied: it is the eaters' right to be served their hearts' desire, and the waiter's job to tell them what that might be. Diners' phobias as well as their predilections are honoured and respected, which ensures that they are served no surprises,
yet get blown away by the eating experience. The fashion in certain upscale joints is for the line chef who cooked a course to serve it to table, all the better to explain to the customer just how great! it's gonna be. In America, anticipation, as well as appetites and portion sizes are huge.

After that diversion, let's consider what we really want from our food stores. Singles nights and special offers are all very well, and, in a competitive market, range, value and service are givens, so what is there left to hope for? The best food shopping is about possibilities, of leaving the shopping list at home and being tempted by what's on offer. Great food stores and supermarkets go even further than that, and act as intermediaries between us and the suppliers. The best remind us constantly of where the food on their shelves has come from: who made it, where, how and why. These stores inform, build and maintain the intimate connection between the food we buy and ourselves.

And because digestion is the last part of food, the best food stores are those who seek to make their produce more digestible, by trading it fairly, so ensuring a mutually honourable outcome to 'la petite bataille.'

A positive food shopping experience is an essential luxury, because eating food is the most intimate thing that we can do with our bodies: it can be more arousing than French kissing, and is more deeply personal than making love. The food that we ingest becomes us – we subsume it, walk around with it, digest its nutrients until there is no difference between it and us – a persuasive argument, if ever there was one, to eat good food that has been responsibly sold.

Let me leave you here with a quote from Khalil Gibran's The Prophet, who, in response to the merchant's question, predicted:

'To you the earth yields her fruit, and you shall not want if you know how to fill your hands.

It is in exchanging the gifts of the earth that you shall find abundance and be satisfied.

Yet unless the exchange be in love and kindly justice it will but lead some to greed and others to hunger.'

# Leif Männerstrøm's seared gravlax

Gravlax is simply salmon fillet in a delicious cure. Whereas Swedish families might once have had to bury their fish to cure it, home refrigeration now renders this charming ritual redundant. And while the fashion for serving smoked salmon roasted has (hopefully) been and gone, top Swedish chef Leif Männerstrøm has found that seared gravlax points up the delicate flavour of the fish, and brings a new dimension to this Scandinavian classic. He serves it with strips of salmon skin, floured and fried to a crisp. You might like to do so as well, in which case, remove the skin from the fish after curing, scrape the scales from it and cut it into thin strips.

serves 4

**preparation 20 minutes, plus 24–48 hours' marinating**

**1 kg salmon fillet, cut from the centre of the fish**

*for the marinade*
**½ cup of light brown sugar**
**¼ cup of fine sea salt**
**a large bunch of dill, finely chopped**
**roughly crushed white pepper**

*for the mustard sauce*
**2 tablespoons French mustard**
**2 tablespoons white granulated sugar**
**1 tablespoon light soy sauce**
**a few drops of Worcestershire sauce**
**a tiny pinch of salt**
**a large bunch of dill, finely chopped**
**½ cup of light vegetable oil**

♥   Combine the marinade ingredients, rub the marinade thoroughly all over the fish, and cover tightly in two layers of cling-film. Leave the fish to cure at the bottom of your refrigerator for at least 24 and up to 48 hours.

♥   Meanwhile, make the mustard sauce by combining all the ingredients except the oil, which should then be slowly whisked in, so creating a delicious thick emulsion. For maximum taste effect, the sauce should be very green. If needed, chop in more dill.

♥   When the fish is ready, remove the skin and cut the cured flesh into large squares.

♥   Heat a griddle pan or dry frying pan until very hot, then briefly sear the pieces of fish.

♥   Serve warm, accompanied by the sauce, the fried skin if using it and, perhaps, the bitter leaves salad on page 136, albeit this time without the green dressing.

# Bülent's 40-day olives

Olives have sustained humans for millennia. Olive trees take seven years to fruit but, when climate, place and care are in harmony, can continue fruiting for 150 years or more. Those of you who have tried to eat an olive direct from the tree will remember that olives must undergo treatment if they are to become good food – straight off the branch, they are extraordinarily bitter. The best olives are the ones that are hand-picked when naturally ripe. This rule makes no distinction between green and black ones, as green olives turn naturally black when left on the tree.

All over Europe, sheets are spread under olive trees to catch fruit that ripens and falls naturally. Ladders are also leant against the gnarly trunks of the trees; the olive picker who climbs among the branches will be expert in knowing which fruit are ready to be coaxed into the harvesting basket and which still need time and warmth if they are to achieve their best. In the name of progress, major table olive manufacturers have developed mechanical methods for stripping unripe green olives from trees, as this reduces labour costs and ensures that trees also offer 100 per cent yields. The problems with this method are, first, that a machine cannot differentiate between an olive that is ready for picking and one that would benefit from a few days' more sunshine and, secondly, that the fruit then needs considerably more rigorous chemical treatment if it is to reach acceptable levels of edibility.

This is particularly true in the processing of 'black' olives. In many cases, these are simply machine-stripped green olives that are then subjected to salt and alkaline baths before being dyed with a ferrous (iron) solution. Any flavour the olive may once have owned disappears like the shadow of a memory in its various soakings and dyeing. It's easy to recognize a dyed olive: its skin is a very uniform black colour, and it exhibits none of the subtle gradations of shade shown in natural olives. Also, its stone, or pit, will have taken up the iron dye and be dark grey in colour; real black olives have brown pits. It is always worth seeking out real olives, and, as the following story shows, they may then benefit from further treatment in your home.

Bülent ... was a Turk who knew the secret of The Way, the name given by Sufis to the Path of Return to God. An antique dealer by trade, his true work was in transforming subtle energies and in guiding others along The Way. He had many followers, whom he formed into a school called Beshara, with centres in the eastern Mediterranean and Scotland. One of his students was a red-bearded ex-stockbroker, ex-pop-musician-turned-healer called Reshad Field. In 1976, Reshad wrote about his encounter with and transformation by Bülent in a book called *The Last Barrier* (see the bibliography at the back of the book). In the mid-1970s it was not yet as fashionable as it is today to discuss spiritual matters openly: for that and other reasons, Bülent's name is rendered as Hamid. Here follows an excerpt from *The Last Barrier*. The scene is a tiny kitchen in a simple house lent to 'Hamid' in Side, southern Turkey, where Reshad (recently arrived from London) is staying to begin his transformation:

'I watched him cutting vegetables by the stove, noting the intensity of each movement that he made. It had been the same in London. He never spoke when he was preparing food, for he said that it was such a sacred act that it was necessary to do everything in awareness and respect. "Be grateful for all that gives you life," he would say, "and make yourself good food for God."

'I ate some of the olives. They were quite extraordinary, unlike any olives I had ever tasted, and I wondered where he had obtained them. When he had finished preparing the food, I asked him about them. "Ah," he said, "to get olives like this requires a very special process." He sat down with me and I poured him some wine. "Let us toast the olives," he said, "for these olives went through a lot to become as delicious as they are." Then he began to laugh, great belly laughs that shook the table. "You had the same olives many times in London," he said. "Why did you not notice them then? But if you had, then maybe you wouldn't have had to come all the way to Anatolia to find out about them.

"To prepare olives like this, the first thing you must do is to buy the very best quality you can find. Then rinse them carefully several times so that all the salt is washed away. You understand?" I nodded, making mental notes so that I could fix some in the same way. "Next, take a jar that you have washed carefully – it must be perfectly clean. Into it put the washed olives, and over the olives pour boiling water. The olives will swell. Leave the water on them just long enough for them to expand – but not too long, or the skins will burst. Then pour away the water and add some slices of lemon and fresh mint. Finally you fill up the jar with first-pressing olive oil, the purest you can find, which is the essence of olives. Screw the lid on the jar very tightly and leave for 40 days and 40 nights. Then they are perfect. Mind you, they are pretty good after seven days!" He roared with laughter again..."'

There is perfect harmony in this recipe. The sweetness of the mint balances the acid of the lemon, which is in harmony with the savoury salt of the olives. In preparing this dish, you may notice that the analogies with the human condition are delectable. In order for transformation to happen, there must often be a cleansing, or de-conditioning, followed by what may seem like harsh treatment (in this case with boiling water). Containment is then inevitable, as is the addition of new 'flavourings', to be followed by immersion in a new essence and, lastly, repose and reflection for 40 days and 40 nights. Mind you, you too can be pretty good after seven days!

## fills a 450g screw-top jar

**preparation 17 minutes, plus 40 days and 40 nights**

250g best (unstoned) olives, black or green
a kettleful of boiling water
2 slices of lemon, cut small
2 sprigs of fresh mint, leaves only
very good extra-virgin olive oil

♥    Place the olives in the jar – they should fill the space by more or less four-fifths. Pour on boiling water to fill the jar, and watch the olives swell.

♥    Before the skins split (between 3 and 10 minutes, depending on the olives, the water and your clock), drain off the water.

♥    Introduce the lemon pieces and the mint leaves and agitate the jar very gently in order to distribute them evenly.

♥    Fill the jar with your olive oil, then fasten the lid tightly.

♥    Leave the olive jar, ideally in a cool dark place (but not in the fridge), for 40 days and nights – if you have the discipline!

# fish and seafood soup garnished three ways

Making great fish soup requires time, expense, expertise and a willing fishmonger. Those of us for whom any of the above may be in short supply could consider instead the purchase of a jar of one of M. Perard's renowned soups, sold in distinctive straight-sided jars in 20 countries. 'I invented fish soup, you know!' Our man has repeated this formula so many times in the last 55 years that he utters it with absolute certainty. Monsieur Serge Perard is an energetic, albeit unconventional, champion of his seafood soup restaurant business in Le Touquet-Paris-Plage, northern France. This small smart, self-satisfied town, for many generations the resort of choice to visitors of quality, is dominated at night by an enormous neon sign: 'Do Not Buy Fish Soup from Perard's Restaurant. All of France Will Demand It!'

Now 80 years old, M. Perard retains a dry sense of humour and a salesman's instincts. His story starts during the Second World War. 'It wasn't Alice in Wonderland, you know,' states Monsieur Serge, 'more like Alice in the Land of Severe Rationing. Fishing was restricted by the soldiers, but my friend Maurice and I went along to the Halles des Poissons in Boulogne-sur-Mer to see what we could scrounge.' Maurice and he saw that fish heads were being discarded, and bought themselves two nice fat ones for a few sous. 'We went home and sated our hunger with a few potatoes and the fish heads, simply boiled in water. I kept some of the boiling stock, and that evening fancied it up with plenty of onions lightly sautéed in thyme, bay, garlic, salt and pepper. Once again' – he pauses to enforce the point – 'we were well entertained by this simple soup.'

For nearly 20 years young Serge was to refine his recipe, waiting for the day when he could introduce all of France to his invention. In the 1960s, eating fish was not in fashion, and no matter its seaside location (promising the most iodized air in France!) and its proximity to Boulogne (the nation's busiest port), Le Touquet boasted not one seafood restaurant. Serge Perard opened his in July 1963, with little money but 'an indomitable liver', serving a curious clientele with his signature soup, by now enriched with crustaceans and saffron.

Restaurant Perard remains in its original premises on Le Touquet's Rue de Metz. It features an abundant wet fish and seafood counter, and an 80-cover restaurant, still dressed in its 1960s livery of puce linen, orange light fittings and a knobbly copper wall that looks for all the world like a giant turbot. It was in his 'Utopia' *chez* Perard that our man with the girded liver made soup to his secret recipe. Before long, customers wanted to enjoy this invention *chez eux*, so Perard went to Paris to learn the conserver's art, and henceforth packaged his soup in a sterilized jar. By 1970, Monsieur Serge's soups, bearing the legend 'Bouillabaisse of the North!' were being jarred at the rate of 3,000 per day, these sales having been achieved only through word of mouth. 'We didn't need salesmen,' says M. Perard, 'the soup sold itself!' *Bien sûr, Monsieur.*

Soup is no longer made on the Rue de Metz – in 1991 its manufacture moved to purpose-built premises on the outskirts of town. 'We had thought of moving the whole operation to Boulogne to be nearer the port, but the mayor of Le Touquet *himself* insisted that I stay, and the municipality granted us land to build on.' The original fish soup has now been joined by crab and lobster versions, each as evocative of the coastal seas and as rich as the other.

*Établissement Perard* invested heavily in new machinery, which has lifted bottling capacity to around 10,000 jars per day, with no discernible change in quality from its artisanal beginnings. The soups are sold to an international clientele. 'They especially like the soup in Saudi Arabia,' offers Monsieur, man to man, 'for its… *énergétique* qualities. People ask me how, at 80 years old, I retain my…. ahem…. enthusiasm for life. I say, "Let them eat soup and find out!"' He doesn't actually say 'oh-eeh-oh', but a nod's as good as a wink.

A bowl of soup eaten *chez* Perard is an unalloyed pleasure. The restaurant plods at a constant assured pace and is staffed, in some cases, by retainers taken on in 1963. Restaurant Perard's period design is accessorized by the accumulation of 40 years of knick-knacks – a photo of Churchill here, some dreadful piscine art there, cartoons of De Gaulle on the wall and sea-green terrazzo tiling underfoot. Amongst all this gaudy bric-à-brac, Perard's Seafood Soups reign supreme. They are borne to table on support-stockinged legs and served with no small hint of reverence.

As a starter, with croutons, grated Gruyère and *rouille*, the fish soup tastes comforting and deeply satisfying, its layers of flavour clarion clear, a testament to its myriad ingredients and oft-repeated recipe. A richer offering is made in Perard's bouillabaisse, the soup bowl piled high with singing-fresh langoustines, dense mussels and palourde clams-a-plenty. Finger bowls are provided, and table manners are somehow held on to, despite the urge to gorge on so immense a seafood-fest. Favoured diners, and those deemed by the matronly staff to be properly appreciative of Monsieur's oeuvre, are treated to seconds of soup ladled from a tureen that passes among the tables.

*Monsieur le patron* is always on hand to receive plaudits. He holds out his hands in an attitude of wry pride. 'I've lived my adult life with this fish soup.' Wait for it. 'I'm not rich, but my soup is!'

Here, then, are three ways to enjoy a densely flavoured seafood soup. Each provides plenty of garnish for 4 people.

## traditional – saffron rouille, Gruyère, croutons

*Rouille* is a flavoured mayonnaise with a taste that appears at first nonchalant, later becoming more ardent:

♥ Steep a pinch of saffron in a tablespoon of boiling water for 10 minutes. Grill a deseeded (sweet or hot, your choice) red pepper, skin it and mash the flesh to a pulp.

♥ Meanwhile, pound 2 garlic cloves in a mortar with half a teaspoon of salt, then stir in the yolks of 2 eggs, followed by the saffron and its water and the pulped pepper.

♥ Whisking constantly with a fork, add light vegetable or olive oil to the mixture, starting a drop at a time, then increasing the flow. By the time you have about 300ml, the *rouille* should be unctuous and thick. (This can easily be done in a food processor, at slow speed.)

♥ *Rouille* ought to be served spread thickly on croutons of baked baguette or ficelle, on top of which is piled grated Gruyère cheese, these boats to be floated on the fish soup and eaten in *stracciatelle* mouthfuls when the crouton sinks, sodden, to the bed of the saffron-flavoured soup. The rouille is best used within 3 days, and must be kept refrigerated.

## bouillabaisse style

Real bouillabaisse, if the Marseillaises are to be believed, should be made by virgins, with only fish caught from an area within view of the old port, to a recipe buried with its inventor, its secret known only to the owner of Chez Bacon and his bank manager. Or something.

You can, however, approximate the dish any time by adding fish and seafood to a fish soup base. Use whatever you can find – clams, prawns, langoustines, mussels, perhaps a few chunks of white fish. Your best bet is to steam the ingredients with a sprinkle of salt over them, while the soup is heating up, then to serve them in the soup, accompanied perhaps by a glass of chilled Bandol rosé, if you're after that authentic Provençal experience.

## roasted fennel rouille

I like this very much. Provençal people love the anis tang of fennel and serve it many ways. For instance, *rougets* (red mullet), stuffed with stalks of dried fennel are flambéed in Pernod to memorable effect. Here's a way of using fresh fennel that accentuates the flavours of both the soup and the rouille.

♥   Roast a large fennel bulb as it is, reserving the stalk and fronds, in a medium oven until soft (around 15–20 minutes).

♥   Meanwhile, pound 2 garlic cloves in a mortar with half a teaspoon of salt. Add 2 egg yolks and beat with a fork, adding 300ml vegetable oil a drop at a time to begin with, then increasing the flow until you have a thick rouille.

♥   Strip the roast fennel of its coarse outer leaves, slice off the base and roughly mash with a fork (or blitz in a processor). Moisten with 1 tablespoon of Pernod, Ricard or Anis. Beat the fragrant mashed fennel into the *rouille* and adjust the seasoning to taste.

♥   Serve simply spooned into the fish soup or on crouton boats.

*Restaurant Serge Perard*
*67 Rue de Metz, 62520 Le Touquet*
*telephone 33 (0) 21 05 13 33*

# Native oysters and French sausages

This dish should more properly be named *huitres à la marennes*. Marennes, a port on the Bay of Biscay, lies south of La Rochelle, its shore protected by l'Île d'Oléron. This stretch of Atlantic France is famous for its oysters, and it was near here, on the Île de Ré, that the art of modern oyster farming was born. Its progenitor was a patient man called Hyacinthe Boeuf (no kidding), a mason who was employed to build the island's walls. For a decade, he observed the tides and the actions of the currents, all the time noting where and when oysters spawned. Hyacinthe bought the rights to a stretch of coast that had easy access and twice-a-day tides, and built a wall to form a reservoir and break the current. Oyster spats grew naturally and abundantly on his wall. Hyacinthe then transferred the baby crustaceans to tiles on which they sat for 18 months, drinking and filtering the plankton-rich Atlantic water before their harvesting.

Hyacinthe Boeuf's method of pisciculture was taken up by many others – and is still practised today – perhaps most notably by the fishermen of Marennes. If oysters are to prosper and grow hardy, they require their beds to be subject to regular tides, which leave the crustaceans exposed to the air (and clamped shut) when they ebb. This strengthens the oyster's muscle, in itself a masterpiece of natural engineering – more intricate than a Swiss watch, more powerful than a mechanical vice. During their 18 months or so on the tiles, oysters undergo what can be called serial hermaphroditism, today a girl, tomorrow a boy, and so on. (How funky is an oyster: this transsexual shellfish, this ladyboy of the lagoon!)

After harvesting, oysters must rest in baths of clean running water for 3 days, during which time they shed any impurities. Clasped tight shut, they retain enough of their native water (liquor) to survive the journey to table. Therefore, the water in which an oyster lives imbues it with its flavour and tang. For this reason, Pacific oysters, raised in warm, salty water, grow huge but can taste thin and harsh. Gigas and natives can be shell-full of flavour, but knowledge of their provenance is essential if disappointment is to be avoided.

Should you be lucky enough to find them, the oysters of Loch Fyne have a special savour and a delicacy all of their own. Loch Fyne runs inland 50 miles on the wet and windy west coast of Scotland. At the head of the loch, Johnny Noble and Andrew Lane have farmed oysters since 1977 in conscious remembrance of the past: oysters were farmed on these shores even during Roman times. Their headquarters are in Johnny's ancestral castle on the loch shore, which gives out over the oyster beds and mussel ropes they have painstakingly laid down.

The waters at the loch head, liberally sprinkled by the 90cm of rain that fall each year, are a happy mixture of Gulf Stream-warmed sea water and the soft peaty burn water from the hills. The result is oysters with a pronounced nuttiness and a sweet, salty savour.

This dish owes much to Loch Fyne, in whose restaurants it is offered. Johnny and Andrew buy their spat from Marennes, and saw how the oystermen would build a small fire and grill themselves small sausages, chased down with icy fresh oysters. The mixture of shapes, flavours, textures and temperatures, you'll agree, makes *huitres à la marennes* a winning combination with sexy connotations.

♥    There's little to the dish in terms of preparation. You'll need only a warm-to-medium oven in which to roast half a dozen best-quality, natural-casing, small pork sausages, such as chipolatas or fresh saucissons (it should take about 20 minutes – do not prick the skins, instead shake the roasting pan from time to time), and a dozen (ideally cold-water) oysters in their shells to serve two lovers. Lemon juice can be a good thing – Tabasco or shallot vinegar, while traditional, tends to mask the flavour of good oysters.

# garlic aubergines, chargrilled courgettes and carrots, baby artichokes and seared onions preserved in oil

These *sott'òlio* are satisfying to make, particularly as they last very well, thus prolonging the pleasure that you can take from them! What sets them apart from shop-bought *sott'òlio* is the good oil that you should use. In each case, the preserves may be held under oil in a shallow bowl. For longer keeping, place them in perfectly clean jars, completely covered by the oil, and screw the lids on tightly – you should find that their flavour improves with keeping. Make these whenever you have the time and a bag full of fresh, in-season produce. Quantities given are only guidelines and can be scaled up and down to match your produce and needs.

**preparation 25 minutes**

**good olive oil**
**sea salt and black pepper**

*for the garlic aubergines*
**2 medium-large aubergines, cut lengthwise into thin slices**
**2 garlic cloves, peeled and halved**

*for the chargrilled courgettes*
**4 small-to-medium courgettes, sliced lengthwise**
**1 teaspoon brown sugar**
**4 tablespoons white wine vinegar**
**1 teaspoon dried thyme**

*for the baby artichokes*
**8 baby artichokes**
**juice of 1 lemon**
**a few strips of fresh orange zest**

*for the seared white onions*
**2 white onions, sliced across**

♥ To prepare the garlic aubergines: rub a thin film of olive oil on a griddle pan and place over a medium heat.

♥ Rub each slice of aubergine with the cut edge of the garlic.

♥ Cook the aubergine on both sides, sprinkling with salt, until marked but not burnt.

♥ Allow the slices to cool down to room temperature, then place under oil with the garlic halves.

♥ To prepare the chargrilled courgettes: cook the courgettes as for the aubergines above and allow to cool down to room temperature.

♥ Bring the vinegar to the boil in a small pan and dissolve the brown sugar in it.

♥ Stir this into about 175ml oil, place the chargrilled courgettes in the oil and mix in the dried herb.

♥ To prepare the baby artichokes: boil the artichokes in salted water with the juice of half the lemon. When soft, remove, sprinkle with the rest of the lemon juice and more salt, then place under oil while the artichokes are still hot. Mix in the orange zest.

♥ To prepare the seared white onions: very lightly oil a non-stick frying pan and place over a high heat. Put the onion rings in the pan a few at a time and turn them after about 30 seconds, seasoning generously with black pepper. Place under oil while still hot.

# Collation of cured and dried meats

A selection of charcuterie, bought fresh from a reputable store with a healthy turnover, offers a range of flavours and textures, and makes an easy dish to serve with drinks and friends. As it's such an easy presentation, why not take the trouble to make some chic accessories?

serves 6

**preparation 20 minutes**

**1.25kg selection of cured, smoked, cooked and dried meats, such as: prosciutto, bresaola, coppa, salami, roast beef, etc., sliced as recently and as thinly as possible**

## accessory 1 - chargrilled pumpkin

♥ Slice 250g orange-fleshed pumpkin, peeled, with seeds and pith removed, as thinly as you can, and toss with a little olive oil.

♥ Lightly oil and heat a griddle pan until it just starts to smoke, then grill each slice of pumpkin for 30 seconds on each side.

♥ Sprinkle with a little balsamic vinegar and some coarse salt.

### accessory 2 – tart grapes:

♥    Add to a cup or so of fresh lemon or lime juice 3 tablespoons (or more) of grappa and a good grind of black pepper.

♥    Soak (all right, macerate) 150g seedless green grapes (the tarter the better), halved, in this for at least an hour, preferably overnight.

### accessory 3 – sumac pistachios

♥    Heat a dry frying pan over a medium-high heat.

♥    Sprinkle 125g shelled pistachios kernels with water, then roll them in 1 tablespoon of sumac (a powder of dried, sour-flavoured berry, available from most Eastern grocery stores) and coarse salt.

♥    Dry-fry, shaking the pan constantly for about 3–4 minutes.

♥    Remove from the pan and let crisp up at room temperature for at least an hour. They will keep indefinitely in a sealed container.

# Quince butter

*Membrillo* to the Spanish, *cotignac* to the French, quince jelly is a gritty garnet-coloured preserve served with hard cheeses and cooked meats. Delicious though it can be, I prefer this American treatment of the quince, a downy-skinned fruit the tantalizing fragrance of which permeates the kitchen. Unopened, the butter lasts for months, providing you make it slowly and your jars are properly sterilized. Alternatively, decant the butter into Tupperware, in which it may be stored, refrigerated, for up to 2 months.

♥    Use as many quinces as you have place for in your pan. Do not trouble to peel or core the fruit, simply cut into even-sized rough chunks. Add nearly enough water to cover and cook until the fruit is very soft, probably about an hour.

♥    Process to a purée, measure the volume and return to the pan with three-quarters the volume of granulated sugar (I use golden granulated to accentuate the cooked quinces' colour). Keeping the heat under the pan low, cook until the mixture is thick, stirring constantly or the mixture will burn. Skim off any scum.

♥    When it is thick, but before it becomes treacly, pour it into Tupperware and refrigerate when cool. Alternatively, pour into sterilized jars, screw on lids and place in a large pan. Half-cover with water and gently bring to the boil. Let boil for 2 minutes, then remove the jars and leave to cool. The resultant preserve should be stable at room temperature; once opened, refrigerate and eat within a few days. Any excuse!

# griddled oatcakes

These oatcakes are quick to make, and are lovely with cheese. Once made, they keep well in an airtight container for up to 2 weeks.

makes 6

**preparation about 1 hour, plus resting and cooling**

250g medium oatmeal, plus more for dusting
50g self-raising flour
1 teaspoon fine salt
50g unsalted butter
about 6 tablespoons boiling water

♥   Place the oatmeal in a bowl and sift in the flour and the salt. Mix together well.

♥   Soften the butter with a fork, then add little by little to the oatmeal mixture, rubbing it in with your fingers. Stir in just enough boiling water to create a soft dough. Turn the dough out on a board dusted with oatmeal or a clean marble slab and knead until smooth. Divide into 6 equal portions, and cover the rest with a damp cloth while you roll each out into as thin a circle as you're able.

♥   Heat a dry non-stick frying pan and drop in the oatcakes, one by one. Cook each over a low heat for about 4 minutes each side, turning once.

♥   Allow to cool, then eat or store

---

# anis-spiked watermelon

They do this in Bulgaria, you know, and (for all I know) in other ex-Soviet satellite states. The idea is to inject a watermelon with enough booze to guarantee that your picnic will go with a swing. Anis (or Pernod/Ricard/Pastis/Raki) reacts brilliantly with the watermelon juices, causing milky veins to course through its pink flesh. For more about syringes, see Tomatoes with a Love Injection on page 59).

♥   Find a watermelon that you hope is sweet. With a syringe, draw out as much juice as you can. Fill the syringe with the anis and inject the melon all over, liberally and often, with the alcohol. Allow the watermelon to rest for at least an hour before cutting it into grin-shaped segments.

# Rococo chocolate sauce over fresh cherries

Chantal Coady has a beautiful chocolate shop on London's King's Road called Rococo. The shop smells so amazingly good that I defy anybody to leave without sampling and buying some of Chantal's artisanal confections.

As well as an incomparable range of single-estate Valrhona chocolates, Chantal also makes her own flavoured organic bars in her tiny workshop. Pouring her finished product into 18th-century French moulds, she combines unusual, often arresting flavours with plain and milk chocolate, including orange and geranium, pink peppercorn, sea salt and chilli pepper! Visit Chantal (unless you are too weak to resist such temptation, or so strong as to be rigid) for an education in the art of the *chocolatier*. Alternatively, buy her beautiful book, *Real Chocolate*, published by Quadrille.

This is an adaptation of Chantal Coady's fast and fail-safe chocolate sauce (which she promises is incredibly healthy, being low in fat and high in pleasure). It makes a large quantity of sauce, which keeps well in a refrigerator to tantalize and torture you.

serves 4

**preparation 10 minutes**

2 bars (probably 170g each) of the best dark chocolate you can find, broken into small chips (we used a mixture of Valrhona #3 Grand Cru Caraïbe 66% and #2 Grand Cuvée Guanaja 70%, from Rococo)
150ml plain clean water
about 30g caster sugar
500g fresh cherries

*Rococo Chocolates*
*321 Kings Road*
*London SW3 5EP*
*www.rococochocolates.com*

💜  Add the chocolate to the water in a small pan and whisk constantly over the lowest possible heat, adding some sugar when the chocolate has all but melted (about 3 minutes). Taste the sauce and adjust for sweetness.

💜  When the sauce is made, pour immediately and with abandon over the fresh cherries.

# chapter three
## kitchen yoga

Yoga is designed to help us achieve a clear, light form of consciousness. There are many schools of yoga discipline, which seem to have become increasingly politicized and, inevitably, polarized. The chatter in the health club wonders if a Hatha teacher can understand the philosophy behind Ashtanga, if Kundalini yoga is safe for pregnant mothers, and so on... This Western need to 'understand' and 'take ownership of' ancient Eastern philosophies divides, diverts and traduces what are essentially simple systems designed as aids to healthy living.

Yoga does not even have to include curious gymnastics – all yogis aspire to, and a group of earthbound angels called the Brahma Kumaris practise, something called Raja yoga, a form of constant, eyes-open meditation.

So, without getting drawn into taking sides with any single school, let's agree that all yogas' intention is to imbue discipline, routine, suppleness and flexibility into the yogi's body and/or mind, with a view to achieving clearer thinking, increased stamina, enhanced energy and, ultimately, enlightenment. In all of these there are parallels with acts of cooking: the practice I'd like to be known from now on as Kitchen yoga.

### DISCIPLINE

The Dalai Lama teaches that discipline is: 'a supreme ornament and, whether worn by the old, young or middle-aged, it gives birth only to happiness. A peerless ointment, it brings relief from the hot pains of delusion.'

What many of us in the freedom-loving West fail to understand fully is that out of apparent constriction comes liberation – that freedom is found only through discipline. Just as the practice of yoga without the discipline of physical and meditative techniques is only disco dancing on a plastic mat, so cooking with reckless abandon is only truly possible within the organized confines of conscious attention. Discipline punctures delusions, its practice breeds control over the body and mind, and without it there can be none of what Tibetans call 'prajna' – the possibility of quality.

Most fundamental of all disciplines is control of the breath. All the major spiritual traditions agree that only by being on top of the breath can we hope to transcend the ordinary and achieve our true potential. Our problem is that we tend to take breathing for granted, to see it as our right to life. (Until we die, that is.) And most forms of yoga require complicated breathing techniques, which can cause intoxication due to oxygen saturation or starvation, particularly if you have your ankles round your ears. We breathe in air and our body takes life from it before expelling the unrequired portion. Panic and stress cause us to 'tighten' in the moment, thus causing restriction of the airways, and reducing the body's ability to rebalance itself.

I believe that cooking only to impress, following unsuitable recipes and cooking while fearing failure all cause tightening, unnecessary panic and stress, with both apparent and hidden consequences. Therefore, there is no better or more important place to practise the discipline of the breath than in the kitchen, where calm leads to positive energy and nurture to nourishment.

Here's the Big Theory on thought eating: water is a conductor of electricity. Not the best conductor, I grant you, but nonetheless an efficient one. Our bodies are made up of 80 per cent water. We breathe in air and breathe it out again, now saturated with minuscule droplets of our essential moisture. Thought forms can be measured as electrostatic impulses. Therefore, we breathe air in and breathe out our thoughts.

Imagine! Not only can you be breathing in other people's thoughts, but you also have the ability to breathe your thoughts into your cooking – which makes it all the more essential to cook with positive thoughts in mind, if your food is to nourish those for whom you cook.

You know well that food made while you are angry, tense or upset never tastes as good as food made in joy. This theory goes as far as to suggest that such unhappy food has a long-term detrimental effect on those who eat it, as 80 per cent of us have the ability to harbour unredeemed thoughts. Therefore, as long as it remains fashionable for celebrity chefs to be shouty and aggressive in their kitchens, I shan't eat their food, for fear of eating hate on a plate.

The positive is that, by conscious breathing, we can not only redeem those thought-forms, but also spread a positive atmosphere around us. The technique to practise is called the Mother's Breath and it is as essential for the sensitive cook as salt or oil. Mother's Breath was refined over many years by the Sufi and geomancer Reshad Field, and is based on one of the great laws of the universe, the Law of Octaves. Details of some of Reshad's books are in the bibliography at the back of the book, but here is a Mother's Breath sampler:

'The practice entails breathing in to a count of seven, pausing for one count, and then breathing out to the count of seven and pausing for one count. The rhythm is the most important thing and not the pace. Each person is unique and should find a pace that they are comfortable with... the first step is to keep the back straight and to watch the breath, in gratefulness to be alive in each moment... [once the rhythm is established and natural] now we can start work with the placing of the breath... breathe in through the body's 'cauldron' – the solar plexus... breathe in what you need for the necessary transformation to take place... we can breathe in earth energy, magnetic energy, colour, vibrations... for the out-breath (on the count of one) raise your attention from the solar plexus to the centre of the chest. At the same time visualize the breath radiating out from that centre in all directions, manifesting as Light.'

The process is to be repeated for the rest of your life. Believe me if you will, the discipline of breathing the Mother's Breath has more to do with the making of good food than just about any other kitchen technique.

## ROUTINE

Like me, you've probably been to yoga classes where the teacher follows a set routine, designed to rebalance the energies while training the system. You know the drill: lie down for a bit, do the Dog, the Archer, the Fish (no need to open and close the mouth like a guppy, love), and so on, then lie down again. In that routine (or however your teacher likes to do things), there is always to be found structure and familiarity, strength and security.

However, familiarity with any routine can cause boredom, the enemy of all cooks. B. K. Iyengar, the yogi who disseminated Hatha yoga throughout the world, describes yoga as 'a living act, not one of mechanical repetition'. Therefore, I suggest elevating kitchen routines to the level of ritual, in an effort to transform the mechanical into the spiritual, and the regular into the special.

This approach, however, is not without its pitfalls. The Dalai Lama warns about the dangers of paying lip service to (food) rituals: 'When you lack the inner dimension for that spiritual experience you are aspiring to, then rituals become mere formalities, external elaborations. In that case, clearly, they lose their meaning and become unnecessary customs – just a good excuse for passing the time. But when through rituals and formalities you create the spiritual space that you are seeking, then the process will have a powerful effect on your experience.'

As in all other forms of yoga, warm-up and warm-down rituals form an essential part of the programme, but are only as useful as the amount of conscious energy that you put into them. Pause first before the act of cooking to take stock of yourself. Become acutely aware of your body, from your fingertips to your toenails and back to the top of your head. Now turn your attention to the breath, remembering the rhythm and intention of the Mother's Breath. When you are fully awake, and acutely aware of all around you, it is time to start. Some of you might offer up a prayer and others, thanks; yet others might always play a track from a favourite CD (Come to think of it, why don't fitted kitchens have sound systems built in? Good music enhances almost any kitchen atmosphere.) By respecting kitchen ritual – taking and making stock of yourself – you make yourself into good food for your Creator.

## SUPPLENESS AND FLEXIBILITY

A supple body and a supple mind offer great opportunities and exhibit great appetites for change. Most people, however, are afraid of change, and seek to hold on to whatever they have, no matter how damaging or unsuitable it may be to them. All Sufi lessons on impermanence revolve around the tenet that change is the only thing that can be guaranteed, that only change is permanent.

B. K. Iyengar, in *Light on Yoga*, is at pains to remind us that suppleness means firmness, that those who are supple are like 'candles that are sheltered from the wind, whose flame does not flicker. Suppleness is equal to firmness of will.' Through discipline and breathing suppleness can be trained into the body. By eating good food, it

becomes a temple, although Iyengar is careful to warn against greed: 'Consume food,' he directs, 'but don't let it consume you.' By applying suppleness to Kitchen yoga, our bodies become temples and the table our altar.

Supple cooks are innovators, ready to question the rules and able to think laterally. Flexibility is about improvisation, creating harmony by using good sense and whatever ingredients are available. Flexible cooks make banquets out of leftovers, a form of reincarnation made food. There is much talk and many questions about reincarnation (a favourite is from Reshad Field, whose rules for fully living life by being alive to every moment include the observation, Reincarnation exists until you know you don't need it!'). The last word, though should go to baseball hero 'Yogi' Berra, who described reincarnation as: 'Like *déjà vu* all over again.'

# tomatoes with a love injection

These 'Cherry Marys' make thought-provoking, mouth-exploding canapés, and are fine sharpeners when served at a Sunday brunch. You will be able to tell a great deal about your guests by the manner in which they eat these whole-food cocktails. Those who pop them immediately, unquestioningly, straight into their mouths and are exhilarated by the dish will generally make more spontaneous lovers than timorous nibblers. Mind you, there's much to be said for the occasional coy nibble!

## makes 12

**preparation 25 minutes**

**12 perfect cherry tomatoes, brought up to room temperature for at least an hour**
**a good pinch of salt**
**juice of ½ lemon**
**200ml good-quality vodka**
**1 tablespoon Worcestershire Sauce**
**1 teaspoon red or green Tabasco sauce**

Hypodermic syringes are easy enough to buy from most pharmacies. Little 10ml syringes are sold over the counter to diabetics – it is better, however, to have a larger syringe if possible. Ask nicely and explain that you're addicted to good living, as opposed to heroin. Make sure that whichever syringe you score has the largest possible diameter needle, as the spicy mixture can gum up the works.

♥ Using an empty syringe, enter each tomato through its green head and remove as much juice as you are able. Keep the juice, if you like, to add to any soup or stock that you might be making.

♥ Dissolve the salt in the lemon juice. Mix this with all the other ingredients and stir very well.

♥ Drain the mixture through a square of muslin or a double thickness of kitchen paper.

♥ Fill the syringe with the filtered liquid and tap it a couple of times to remove any air bubbles and to appear professional.

♥ Inject a small amount through the green head into each tomato – take care, though, inject too much and the skin will split; you'll need less than you think.

♥ Chill, if you have the time, for an hour or so, before your guest arrives.

♥ Serve with small napkins, as the tomatoes can spurt alarmingly!

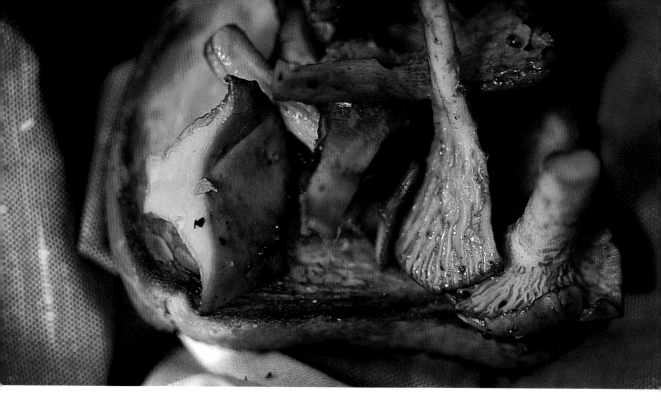

# wild mushrooms on toast

Grilled brioche makes a more thoughtful offering than plain old toast and pays due respect to the wild mushrooms. I suggest chanterelles: their name alone sings of the forest. In sunny pretty Munich, one day in July, there were stalls overflowing with *Pfifferlingen*, all calling out (in forest language, of course) for a quick jump into the sauté pan with good butter and a few chopped pale-green celery leaves...

### serves 2

**preparation 30 minutes**

2 thick slices of brioche or cholla
about 50g unsalted butter
100g chanterelles, woody feet
removed, if necessary
freshly ground sea salt and black
pepper
1 tablespoon very finely chopped
celery leaves (of as pale a green
as possible)

♥ Toast one side of the bread under the grill. Leave the grill on, as you'll be needing it again in just a few minutes.

♥ Spread butter on the untoasted side and reserve.

♥ Heat about 2 tablespoons of the butter in a medium-hot large frying pan. As soon as it stops foaming, throw in the chanterelles and stir well. Season with salt and pepper, and cook slowly for about 3 minutes, until the mushrooms are cooked and soft, but not coloured.

♥ Grill the buttered bread until it is sizzling all over. Meanwhile, add the celery to the mushrooms and cook for another few seconds.

♥ Pile the chanterelles over the golden bread and eat immediately (singing the song of the forest, of course!).

# minestrone with Parmesan and pesto

There are so many versions of minestrone around that I hesitated before including this one. Good food is so much more than the sum of its ingredients, and the spirit of this autumn soup is in the memory of laughter-filled Sunday lunches, of leftovers reheated for comforting Monday suppers, of kitchen warmth and that happy, safe feeling I get from eating this homely *minestra*.

There are those who enrich the soup by adding a ham bone, or some squares of pancetta, but I don't. There are still others who insist that tomatoes go into minestrone – for me they taste too acid, what with the pesto at the end, but maybe they won't to you. Do not, therefore, be a slave to these ingredients: omit what you will, and use what you find while out shopping or in raiding the larder. Also, this soup somehow tastes better for having been made the day before.

serves 6–8

**preparation 1 hour**

sea salt and freshly ground black pepper
250g pumpkin, peeled, deseeded and depithed, and cut into chunks
250g (about 4 medium) potatoes, diced and rinsed
150g frozen broad beans
125g frozen peas
200g cooked chestnuts (from a jar or a vacuum pack)
400g can borlotti or cannellini beans
1 large onion, chopped small
about 3 tablespoons olive oil
2 celery stalks, chopped small
1 large carrot, diced small
3 tablespoons finely chopped parsley
125g Arborio rice
fresh basil pesto, to serve
coarsely grated Parmesan, to serve

♥ In a large pan, bring plenty of salted water to the boil. Add the pumpkin, potato, broad beans, peas and chestnuts. Simmer for about 45 minutes – all the vegetables should have become very soft – then add the canned beans.

♥ While the soup is simmering, fry the onion in the olive oil until it starts to soften. Add the celery, carrot and parsley, and continue to cook, moistening if necessary with a spoonful or two of the soup. After all, you don't want the vegetables to burn or colour, simply to become very soft.

♥ Add the contents of the frying pan to the soup and taste for seasoning. (This is the point at which the soup should be left if it is to be eaten the next day.)

♥ Bring the soup to the boil and add the rice. Cook for about 20 minutes, until the rice is soft, but not mushy.

♥ Serve with bowls of pesto and Parmesan for your family and friends to help themselves.

# cream-free creamy linguine with clams

Veneto is the region of north-east Italy described by the rivers Po and Tagliamento, and bordered above by the breathtaking peaks of the Dolomite mountains. Veneto is a self-sufficient land. Its capital, Venice, mainly farms tourists nowadays, while the rest of the region is famous for many foods which are treated with a deceptively simple deftness of touch.

As one would expect, fish and seafood are here in abundance – baby crabs and cuttlefish, shellfish soup and wine-stewed eels. Notable is *pesce in soar*, a sweet-and-sour fish dish, the pine nut and raisin embellishment of which echoes across the centuries to times past, when Venice enjoyed preferential trading rights with the Byzantine Empire.

Locally grown rice is turned into *risotto all'onda*, 'with waves', so saturated with liquid that a shaken plate runs ripples across its surface. The Veneto city of Verona is the home of potato gnocchi, and Treviso and Chioggia grow the finest bitter salads (see page 136), while the hill-town of Este, just up from Padua, is famous for its *colomba*, a light-as-air dove-shaped yeasted Easter cake.

Michele Franzolin comes from Este. Now in his mid-30s, he was apprenticed at the town's best-loved restaurant, Il Gambero. As Michele says, 'There are fancier restaurants all over the Veneto, and much more expensive ones, too, but the cooking at Il Gambero is all about love.' He has a theory that food from de luxe restaurants becomes muted and restrained because their ingredients are so expensive that the kitchen cannot afford to make any mistakes. 'At Il Gambero, I learned my cooking with a limited selection of ingredients, none of which you could call grand, and was allowed to make mistakes. But –' he pauses – 'I was encouraged always to translate my passion for food into love. My boss used to say that if I couldn't love what I was cooking, how could the customers be expected to love it either?'

This is Michele's version of *linguine alle vongole*. You'll notice first that it is *in bianco*, i.e. uses no tomato, and secondly that it enriches itself with a sauce that looks and feels like cream, but actually comes from the pasta's starch. It's worth making a good amount of the chilli in oil condiment as it keeps for a couple of weeks in the refrigerator, after which the oil will take on a certain chilli warmth.

**serves 2**

**preparation 15-20 minutes**

about 350g dried linguine

salt

2 tablespoons olive oil

500g clams in the shell (if you can find them, fresh cockles also work very well)

1 small red chilli, deseeded, pith removed, cut into thin ribbons and held in olive oil

1 garlic clove, thinly sliced and held in olive oil

a wine glass of simple crisp white wine (Soave is what is made around Este)

1 teaspoon finely chopped parsley, to garnish

♥ Cook the pasta in plenty of boiling salted water until tender but still firm to the bite (use the cooking time on the packet as a guide).

♥ About 5 minutes before the pasta is due to be ready, heat a dry frying pan over a high heat. When very hot, add the olive oil, followed immediately by the clams. Shake the pan constantly and keep it off the heat. The clams should start to open almost immediately. After 30 seconds or so, add the chilli and the garlic, then throw in the wine and return to a medium heat. Remove the clams that have already opened, or they will overcook.

♥ When the pasta is cooked, drain it, but reserve about 2 tablespoons of the cooking water, which you might yet need to moisten the finished dish. Add the cooked pasta to the pan, and mix it well with the well-flavoured clams. Remove the pan from the heat and add the reserved opened clams.

♥ With a pair of kitchen tongs, rub the pasta/clam mixture in a vigorous zig-zag movement. This encourages the pasta to give up its starch, which you will see gathering at the bottom of the pan, looking like cream. If there's less than about 2 tablespoons of this liquid, add the reserved cooking water.

♥ Serve immediately, with a sprinkling of parsley (and a big thank you to Michele!)

# no-salt massaged shoulder of lamb

An Armenian whose father had served in the first democratic Turkish parliament, Haçik Keshisian and his family landed up in London, where, towards the end of his life, he ran a modest kebab shop in Camden Town. Pam Pam (named after an Armenian allegory for the act of love) was a magnet for food lovers.

Service was never fast and often eccentric, but the tiny storefront was usually crammed with patient customers who would while away the wait alternately drinking in the savoury aroma of sizzling lamb and dipping hot pitta bread into Haçik's incomparably creamy *mança*, a mezze of strained, beaten yoghurt, briefly introduced to a clove of garlic before uniting with the chopped leaves of greenest baby spinach.

'Shoulder!' Haçik would point to his own broad, brawny specimen for emphasis. 'That's where the bloodyhell best flavour is!' Head shaking in admiration of the beauty that would become his creation, Haçik would then demonstrate how this cheap cut of lamb needs special attention if it is to achieve its full flavour potential.

'Relax the meat. Make it very ready for you. Take the flavourings and push and rub, like this...' His concentration was absolute – this man was doing more than simply cooking supper, he was uniting with it – communing is not too loaded a word to describe the affectionate attention he would pay to his ingredients. Winking, Haçik vouchsafed one day that the secret of his cooking was the same

as that of his happy marriage. 'Only I don't, you know, kiss the food, mygod!'

This recipe is inspired by and dedicated to the fond memory of Haçik Keshisian, who died in 1992, having served so many such heavenly food.

This dish is a pleasure to eat with Egyptian Rice with Vermicelli (page 93).

### serves 4

**preparation 2 hours, plus 15 minutes' resting**

2 garlic cloves
juice of 1 lemon
3–4 tablespoons olive oil
black pepper
1 boned lamb shoulder (about 2 kg)
a bunch of mint, roughly chopped
1 tablespoon vinegar

Notes:

1 Skewering meat to test for doneness doesn't count as acupuncture.

2 Giving the meat a VIP topless massage might make you feel better, but is unlikely to improve its final flavour significantly.

3 The flavourings used may be replaced with an Oriental mix of groundnut oil, lemon grass, chilli and basil. However, take advice before attempting a Thai full-body massage.

♥ Preheat the oven to 230°C. Slice the garlic cloves in half and rub the meat all over with the cut ends. Moisten the mint with lemon juice and olive oil and grind a few turns of the pepper mill over it.

♥ Lay the meat fat side up. Slowly and methodically, start to massage this aromatic mixture into the meat with your fingertips. Allow at least 10 minutes for this and let your own stresses disappear with your kneading and pinching movements. Turn the meat over and repeat the massage, remoistening the mixture as you need.

♥ Spread the minty mixture all over the joint, then roll it lengthwise. Tie it with cut pieces of trussing string, securing it with four slip knots. Link the slip knots together top and bottom with a continuous length of string and tie off. Place the joint on a rack in a roasting tin containing a cup of water and put in the preheated oven. Immediately reduce the heat to 220°C and roast for 30 minutes.

♥ Baste the meat well with the pan juices, turn it over and lower the heat to 180°C. If the juices in the pan are burning, add a further cup or so of hot water to them. Roast for another hour or so.

♥ Remove from the oven and let the joint rest, loosely covered in foil, for 15 minutes. Pan juices should be skimmed of fat (just lay a double thickness of kitchen paper over, then discard), deglazed with the vinegar and bubbled in a saucepan so they reduce.

♥ Remove the string from the joint and serve it sliced, with its juices, and perhaps the Egyptian Rice with Vermicelli on page 93.

# fresh ravioli stuffed with prayers

A recipe for success, if that is what you pray for, and a lovely way to spend a contemplative time in the kitchen. Remember, though, that while it is good to have wishes and essential to have hopes, you will not always get what you want, although you will usually get what you need.

I have borrowed the dough recipe from Claudia Roden's lovely peripatetic *The Food of Italy*. The notion of writing on eggs flows from the Sufi healing practices that require Divine affirmations, *suras* from the Holy Qur'àn and some of the many names of God to be written on fabric and worn, or written with vegetable dye on parchment, then washed off and drunk.

In our case, take four perfect fresh eggs for the pasta dough and write your prayer on the shell of each. Leave the eggs somewhere cool and safe (but not in the refrigerator) for at least 1 hour, preferably overnight, wrapped in a clean handkerchief.

serves 4 hungry people

**preparation about 1 hour, plus resting**

*for the pasta dough*
**about 400g soft, fine plain white flour (type 00 is best, if you can find it)**
**a pinch of salt**
**4 perfect fresh eggs as opposite**

*for the filling*
**250g courgettes, peeled and cut into dice**
**1 medium carrot, peeled and cut into small dice**
**a little butter, plus more to serve**
**250g ricotta (cow, buffalo or sheep)**
**50g freshly grated Parmesan, plus more to serve**
**sea salt and freshly ground black pepper**
**a few sesame seeds**
**Fail-safe Tomato Sauce (page 93), to serve (optional)**

♥ First make the pasta dough: put the flour in a big bowl with the salt and make a well in the centre. Break in the eggs and work the flour into the eggs, first with a fork then with your hands. Continue until the ingredients are well mixed, adding a little extra flour if necessary, so that the mass holds together.

♥ Knead for 10-15 minutes until the dough is smooth and elastic, adding a little more flour if the mixture is sticky. Use this kneading time well - reflect on your prayer!

♥ Wrap the dough in cling-film and leave to rest for 15-30 minutes at room temperature before rolling out.

♥ Divide the dough into two balls for ease of handling. Roll each out as thinly as possible through a hand-cranked pasta maker (in which case, run each sheet through twice or more to get it good and thin) or on a lightly floured surface with a lightly floured rolling pin, working from the centre outwards. Experience is the best teacher, so make the recipe (and your prayers) often and well; fairly thin sheets of pasta rolled to an even thickness are the ideal you are hoping for. Again, use the rolling time to contemplate your prayer.

♥ Leave the pasta sheets to rest for 20 minutes.

♥ Meanwhile prepare the stuffing: sauté the diced courgettes and carrots in a little butter until soft.

♥ Gently mash the courgettes and the carrot with the ricotta, Parmesan and any butter left from the sautéing process. Season with salt and a little pepper.

♥ On one sheet of dough, lay heaped tablespoon-sized lumps of the filling at regular intervals.

♥ Into each pile of filling, secrete a single sesame seed and repeat your prayer.

♥ Lay the second layer of dough on top and press well with your fingers around each filling to stick the dough together.

♥ Cut around each bulge of filling with a pastry cutter or sharp knife, taking care not to get too close to the filling. Let the ravioli rest for an hour or so.

♥ Boil the ravioli, a few pieces at a time, in lightly salted, gently boiling water or stock for no more than 4 minutes, or until just tender.

♥ Serve with butter and Parmesan, or with Fail-safe Tomato Sauce.

# bread sown with many seeds, Armenian lavash

This type of flat bread was born in Armenia and has travelled throughout the Caucasus and Asia Minor. In homes and kebab shops alike, it is employed as plate, tablecloth and napkin; when warm it has a delicious suppleness of texture and flavour. It is an instant food, and therefore does not keep.

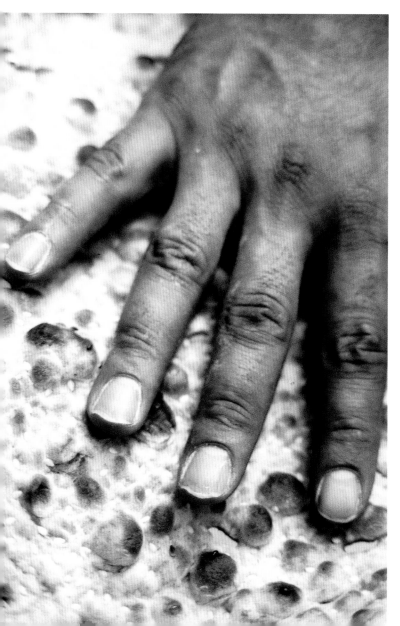

**makes 10**

**preparation 30 minutes**

2 cups of unbleached flour
1 teaspoon salt
2 cups of lukewarm water
about 2 tablespoons sesame seeds
about 2 tablespoons other seeds,
    perhaps nigella, caraway or fennel

♥ Put flour and salt in a bowl. Add the water bit by bit and work in by hand until you achieve a moist dough. Turn out on a floured board and knead for 7 minutes.
♥ Divide into about 10 equal portions, form each portion into a ball and roll out into a rough circle. Sprinkle a handful of seeds over each bread and run over lightly with the roller to embed them.
♥ Place a dry large non-stick frying pan over a high heat, then prick each *lavash* all over with a fork or spiked roller.
♥ Put each *lavash* in the hot pan, un-seeded side down first, and cook for about a minute on each side, shaking the pan the whole time to prevent sticking or burning.
♥ Mottled brown and pale taupe, these *lavash* should be served while (like you!) still warm and supple.

# moon-cycle cowberries

Cowberries (also called lingonberries) are known to Swedish people as the 'red gold of the forest'. This simple recipe, adapted from *The Swedish Kitchen*, works beautifully with cowberries, loganberries, blackberries and raspberries. If you find yourself with a glut of such fruit, rinse briefly and drain well, then freeze in small batches and defrost to turn them into this uncooked compote. *The Swedish Kitchen* points out that berries frozen for more than 3-4 months develop an even sharper (than their already pointed) flavour. The idea here, though, is to mature the compote over one complete cycle of the moon to a) allow the flavours to marry, and b) prove that you have the strength not to open the jar before then!

Makes about 2½ litres

**2 kg (about 3 litres/12 cups) well cleaned berries**
**6 cups of white granulated sugar**

♥ Place the berries in a large bowl (not one made of plastic – the berry juice will stain it). Add the sugar and stir with a wooden spoon or plastic spatula, until the sugar is dissolved and the berries are lightly crushed.

♥ Pour into cold sterilized glass jars, with a little of the residual juice poured in last to cover.

♥ Seal and keep in the fridge for one cycle of the moon, or until your astrologer/conscience allows you to open them.

♥ This compote is very good with thick cream and good friends, or to complement rich savoury dishes, such as roast duck or wild game.

# rice pudding brûlée with caramelized apricots

serves 6

**preparation about 1¼ hours**

3 stoned fresh apricots or 6 dried
   apricots sliced
90g short-grain rice
750ml fresh milk
50g white granulated sugar
6 tablespoons (or so) of caster
   sugar

♥  If using dried apricots, reconstitute them in just-boiled water for 15 minutes, then drain and dry.

♥  Boil the rice in 300ml water for 12–15 minutes, until tender but not mushy.

♥  Add the milk and cook at a bare simmer for 45 minutes, stirring occasionally.

♥  Add the granulated sugar and stir well.

♥  Preheat the grill to medium-high. Drain and slice the dried apricots, if using them; halve, stone and slice the fresh.

♥  Pour the rice mixture into individual ovenproof bowls or ramekins (if doing everything up to this stage in advance, reheat the rice puddings in a microwave or oven before the next step).

♥  Arrange the slices of fresh or dried apricot on top of each bowl and sprinkle with the caster sugar.

♥  Position about 10cm under the preheated grill and grill until the top is bubbling and caramelized. Alternatively (and much better), set about the apricots with a miniature blow-torch (without which no serious cook's kitchen is complete!)

♥  Serve immediately.

# chapter four
## food with families and friends

Cooking is like practising a language. There are so many variations of accent, inflection and idiom, and so many people willing to teach you their own versions of it, that it's easy to forget your own style. Making food for family and friends is an opportunity like no other to say what you mean and to mean what you say – to drop a few metaphorical 'h's and use a bit of slang, maybe – and to express your feelings in your own language. Sophia Loren (an international language in her own right) once said that cooking for her family was like: 'learning to conjugate the verb "to love"'.

Loving and cooking both start with an invitation. For me, a big bowl of pasta with Frances's version of Fail-safe tomato sauce (page 93) is an offer I can never pass up, but in earlier, courtlier days, the invitation to eat was more formalized. Here are a few lines from 'Abd al-Aziz ibn al-Qabturnuh, who wrote and ate in the early part of the 12th century in Badajoz, Spain:

A morning damp with dew
and the earth's cheek
covered with green stubble.
Your friend invites you

To enjoy two simmering pots
already giving off
a savoury odour,
Some perfumes
a carafe of wine
a delicious place,

And I could offer more
if I wanted to;
but it's not seemly to entertain friends
with too much pomp.

Old 'Abd al-Aziz sets the right tone – if you're his real friend, then the highest honour he can pay you is informality. The modern paradox is that the cult of the casual has blurred social boundaries so that, perversely, an open honest invitation to friendship can be perceived as embarrassing, an attempt at 'unwelcome contact'. We may now dress down to work, even take our dog into the office on Fridays, but all this informality seems to keep us from getting to know each other at anything other than a superficial level. What are we all afraid of? That our mystique will be punctured, our façade exposed as veneer, our cover blown – by the warmth of a welcome?

In order to stop it getting recklessly out of hand, the art of hospitality has been formalized and turned into a science that is taught in college. Hospitality is to be encouraged, of course, and, yes, its seeds must be sown and grown in our children, but the subtle art of selflessness comes from within, not from the lecture theatre. Conviviality cannot be taught! Hospitality starts in the heart and is formed in the kitchen, the heart of any home.

By the way, what do you think about the luxury apartments being sold in New York that have no kitchen? I once mentioned the concept to a Camembert maker in

Isigny, Normandy. 'C'est Affreux!' He was horrified and literally had to sit down to recover. 'But… how will people live?' 'Oh, you know,' said I. 'On takeaways, eating out, snacks and the like.' 'Yes, yes, –' impatiently – 'but how will they get their nourishment?' Pierre Bruno's point was a fine one. The heat of the kitchen infuses a home with warmth, and conversation at table feeds that warmth, transforming the food into a form of pure nourishment that does more than simply sustain the system. This nourishment does more than support life: it makes it worth living.

With families and friends, the soul of a relationship is in food shared, and the memories evoked by communal meals. For my brothers and myriad cousins, the spirit of our childhood home is conjured in Friday night dinners, bad jokes and mad laughter, and the tantalizing smell of steaming-hot, saffron-scented rice. Mevlana Rumi, in a beautiful quatrain, sighs at being sent skywards by the scent of a soul, and compares it to the soul of the rose, whose intoxicating essence is love. My Mum's love sustained her to cook for hours and hours. I reckon that (in addition to the aroma of eglantine), Marlene's soul smells of her home-welcoming chicken soup!

Cooking for and eating with kids is a positive way of showing love, and invites them to an appreciation of good food. In purely mechanical terms, cooking for family and friends is a microcosm of the reciprocal maintenance on which the world depends: the world needs to be fed and loved, just as we do. And there's no tastier way to conjugate the verb 'to love'!

# baby cod with fasioi

Michele Franzolin's (see page 64) mother taught him how to make the *fasioi* that underpin this dish. *Fasioi* in the Veneto dialect literally means 'beans', but is more usually used to describe recooked beans. Even though Venice was, in the Middle Ages, the most powerful trading nation in the world, little has remained of the grand dishes feasted on by the Doges and mercantile families who lived in sumptuous canal-side palazzos. Instead, the cooking of the Veneto is characterized by '*la fantasia dei poveri*', the imagination of the poor, who scraped a simple living from the land, and whose clean, simple, honest cooking now best represents the region. Michele uses *merluzo* (baby cod) for this dish: older fish or hake will do. Michele's mother, Giovanna, uses *fagioli perla*, tiny locally grown cannellini beans, although any cannellini or haricot would be almost as delicious.

serves 4

**preparation 1½ hours, plus soaking and cooling**

2 tablespoons olive oil
4 portions of cod fillet, each about 200g, skin on
a good knob of butter
1 tablespoon chopped parsley

*for the beans*
4 cups of cannellini beans (ideally *fagioli perla*, as above), soaked for 24 hours
1 carrot, diced
1 celery stalk, diced
1 onion, diced
sea salt and freshly ground black pepper
a little good oil, to dress (optional)
1 teaspoon chopped parsley, to dress (optional)

♥ First prepare the beans: drain them, put in a pan and cover with cold water to the level of the beans plus 2 fingers. A richer offering could be made by cooking them in stock. Add the vegetables, then cook at a low boil for 1 hour. The beans should absorb all the water, but must remain moist – add more water if necessary (the idea, when they're cooked, is for them to be the consistency of a very thick soup). When the beans are very soft, taste and season.

♥ Allow the beans to cool in what remains of their stock. (Michele's mum lets them cool for at least 24 hours.)

♥ Before serving, reheat well, crushing the beans lightly with the back of a spoon. Michele adds extra flavour by running a little good oil through the beans, with a teaspoon of chopped parsley.

♥ Heat a dry frying pan until just beginning to smoke. Add 2 tablespoons of oil and place the fish in the pan, skin side down. The idea is to cook the fish all the way through, but not so much that it dries out. Michele allows about 2 minutes on each side, rolling the fish ever so gently with a spatula to prevent it sticking to the pan.

♥ When the fish is just cooked, add a good knob of butter to the hot pan, allowing it to brown to the colour of hazelnut shells (in French, *beurre noisette*) and run it around the fish.

♥ Place the fish on top of the beans, surrounded by the chopped parsley. Pour over any remaining brown butter.

# Machiko Jinto's pot-au-feu au fish

Machiko Jinto designs clothes with an incomparable sense of chic, shape and shade. Her work is informed by masterful cutting techniques coupled with inventive use of texture and an eye sensitive to colour contrasts. In her personality and her work, as in her cooking, is the atmosphere of poise and passion, coupled with a kind and ready sense of humour. Machiko is married to Max Rutherston, a specialist in Japanese art for an international auction house.

Their wedding took place in the early-15th-century setting of the chapel at New College, Oxford, where Max had once been a student. In a traditional wedding dress of cream silk, Machiko moved gracefully down the aisle, borne on feet the congregation could not see: the effect was that she was gliding or, more exactly, floating towards the altar. Bright as a jewel in the candlelit church, her elegant outfit was accented and reflected across cultural boundaries in the formality of the El Greco Christ hung behind the choir. The couple now have a beautiful bilingual daughter, Tatyana, and divide their time between an apartment in central Tokyo and a pretty Queen Anne house in London.

Max and Machiko both love to eat *nabe*, and serve the dish to guests from both East and West. *Nabe* is, if you like, Japanese fondue. A communal pot of glazed earthenware is placed in the centre of the table and kept warm by means of a portable gas ring. Into a prepared *dashi* (stock) are placed the ingredients for the meal which, when cooked, are eaten with condiments laid out at each place setting. *Nabe* meals comprise whatever is available to the cook: chicken and vegetables, oysters and spring onions, chargrilled fish and lobster, or *shabu shabu* – wafer-thin slices of marbled beef. Nothing is wasted in *nabe* meals – the fragrant stock that cooks the ingredients then becomes the base in which rice or noodles are cooked with a beaten egg. The result, sometimes called Japanese risotto, is rich with the memory of its preceding ingredients, yet vanishingly light.

*Nabe* style is perhaps the most approachable technique in the Japanese repertoire. Japanese cooking reveres the art and craft of preparation, and some cutting and heating techniques are ritualized and involved; it can therefore appear daunting to Westerners. What is important, though, in *nabe* (as in all cooking, now I think of it) is not a slavish adherence to a set of cultural references, but instead an attitude of consciousness in which careful concentration imbues the act of cooking, and hence the food that is served. It is through this constant attention that any meal is made delicious and digestible. Any good cook follows recipes with precision and produces good results.

Cooking with abandon requires something more – the ability to improvise, to be sure, but also the addition of positive emotion to the process. Only then does a dish become great, and its cook an alchemist whose food has value greater than the sum of its ingredients.

You can serve *nabe* as a cultural set piece, to be cooked clad in a kimono and eaten to the sounds of a *koto* whilst perched on tatami mats that will make your knees ache. More appropriate, perhaps, is to approach *nabe* simply as an exotic pot-au-feu, a cross-cultural opportunity to nourish and entertain, and to cherish your guests.

## serves 4

**preparation 50 minutes**

*for the nabe*

1 carrot, cut into slices (perhaps as flowers with 'petals' cut out)
400g very fresh white fish, such as cod, monkfish etc., or a mixture, cut into bite-sized pieces
150g fresh tofu, cut into even cubes
8 uncooked king or tiger prawns
12 clams or cockles in the shell
a few mangetout (with 'v's cut out, if you like, to look like blades of grass)
8 shiitake mushrooms (perhaps decorated with an 'x' on each cap)
1 cup of oyster or other mushrooms, thickly sliced
1 small head of Chinese leaves, chopped to bite-sized proportions
1 cup of herbs, including *mitsuba* (winter chrysanthemum) if available, or parsley or coriander or chervil if not, heads or sprigs intact but stalks removed
Japanese chives (*nira* or green baby spring onions), snipped

♥ First make the *dashi* stock: place the *kombu* in 2 litres of cold water and bring to the boil. Just before the water boils, remove the *kombu* and reserve for another day, if you like. With the water on a low boil, add the shaved bonito and stir well.

♥ Cook, barely boiling, for 15 minutes, then remove and discard the bonito. The resultant liquid is your *dashi* stock.

♥ While the *dashi* is cooking, prepare the condiments: mix the daikon with the *nira* or spring onions and arrange a small pile at each place setting. Also offer each guest a lime half and a dipping bowl filled with half a cup of *ponzu* sauce.

♥ Heat the stock before bringing it to the table, then place the *nabe* on a table-centre heater, maintaining a low simmer.

♥ Add the ingredients, starting with those that will take the longest time to cook, as listed.

♥ When all the ingredients are cooked (within 3 minutes), guests pick out their favourite tid-bits, dipping them first in *ponzu*, then in the daikon condiment.

♥ When all the *nabe* ingredients are consumed, make the risotto: add the cooked rice to the remaining stock still at table.

♥ As the heat comes up and the dashi starts to bubble, the beaten egg is stirred in with a pair of chopsticks and the heat turned off (otherwise the egg goes too hard) and left to stand for two minutes for a *stracciatella* effect.

♥ Stir in the *nira* and the *nori*, if using.

♥ The intention is to serve a fairly 'wet' risotto, perfumed by the dashi and enriched with the egg.

*for the dashi stock*
1 strip of *kombu* (kelp)
2 cups of shaved dried bonito

*for the condiments*
75g daikon (white radish, also
   known as mooli, and often
   available in ethnic
   groceries), grated very small
   (Machiko sometimes makes
   a hole in the centre of the
   daikon, into which she inserts
   a strip of red pepper, turning
   the grated vegetable an
   alluring shade of pink)
finely chopped *nira* or spring
   onions
2 limes
a bottle of *ponzu* sauce (a
   light soy-based dipping
   sauce with a pronounced
   citrus accent)

*for the risotto*
6 cups of cooked rice
1 egg, lightly beaten
1 tablespoon chopped *nira* or
   green baby spring onions
strips of dried *nori* (dried
   seaweed sheets) to garnish,
   if you like

Machiko Jinto's flagship
store is called Taffeta.
6-2-2 Minami-Aoyama
Minato-Ku
Tokyo 107-0062
Telephone +81 (0)3 5464
3560

# onion-smothered chicken with sharp lemon and hamine eggs

There is a certain elegance in using simple ingredients. I don't mean in terms of dainty presentation – I'm not a great one for all that – but in the luxury of clear flavours, distinct and layered, yet forming part of a harmonious whole. Christian Dior defined elegance with characteristic *élan*: 'Elegance is within the reach of every woman without spending extravagant sums ... if she adopts essential rules of fashion and sticks to choosing clothes which suit her personality. Simplicity, good taste and care are the basic rules of elegance and these three principles are priceless.' As in dressing, so in cooking. This North African dish is an example of such innate refinement.

serves 4

**preparation 1½ hours, plus cooking the eggs**

1 chicken, around 1.5 kg, cut into 8
a little vegetable oil
3–4 lemons
sea salt and freshly ground black pepper
4 large onions, sliced into rings (keep the skins for the eggs)
1 teaspoon toasted sesame seeds

*for the Hamine eggs*
4 eggs
the skins from at least 4 onions, or as many as you can accumulate
1 teaspoon instant coffee (optional, if short on onion skins this enriches the colour)
a little vegetable oil

So rich a dish needs a plain partner – Egyptian rice with vermicelli (page 93), good bread or plain couscous.

♥ Make the hamine eggs well ahead: place the eggs with the onion skins and coffee (if using it) in a large pan. Fill almost to the top with water and set over a very low heat, ideally with a heat diffuser. Float a thin layer of oil on top of the water to help slow evaporation. Cook, covered, at a bare simmer for at least 6 hours, preferably overnight.

♥ In a heatproof casserole, fry the chicken gently in oil until light golden all over. Add water to cover and the juice of 2 lemons. Season and set, covered, over a low heat, barely bubbling, for 45 minutes.

♥ Reserve 4 of your most beautiful onion slices and fry the rest in oil with a good grind of pepper. The idea is to cook the onions slowly, so they become sweet and meltingly soft. Therefore, add water by the spoonful to slow down the cooking and stop the onions burning.

♥ When the onions are very floppy but not yet coloured, add them to the chicken. Cook, uncovered, for another 15 minutes or so, until the liquid has reduced somewhat. The onions will by now be almost disintegrated, the chicken cooked right through, its smaller joints starting to fall off the bone. You might like to cook the dish further, thus making the flesh very soft – it's up to you.

♥ Taste the sauce; if it is too sweet, add more juice from the remaining lemon and cook for another 5 minutes.

♥ Halve a lemon and place the cut sides on a hot griddle pan. Chargrill the 4 reserved onion slices.

♥ Serve the chicken, surrounded by eggs, the charred lemon halves and the onion slices, and sprinkled with the sesame seeds.

# burghul pilaf with halloumi and fresh dill

Lovely and very easy, this is good enough to eat by itself with a salad, or Fail-safe Tomato Sauce (page 93), or No-salt Massaged Shoulder of Lamb (page 66).

serves 4-6

**preparation 40 minutes**

4 cups of medium burghul (cracked wheat), rinsed and drained
6 cups of lightly salted boiling water or stock
2 cups of cubed halloumi cheese, rinsed and drained
1 cup of finely chopped fresh dill
a small knob of butter, if you like

♥ Add the burghul to the liquid, cover the pan and cook over a low heat for 10 minutes.

♥ Remove from the heat and fork in the halloumi, dill and the butter, if using.

♥ Replace the lid and leave to rest and swell for 10–15 minutes more.

♥ Fork through again and serve.

# good-luck lentils

Once upon a time, I was a grocer. My store sold beautiful food from all over the world, all of it produced with integrity, much of it produced by artisans in very small production. Because I love food, the store became a food lover's fantasy. Customers would come in to sample the fresh olives or to taste the farm-made cheeses, or simply for a short holiday from the day, during which time the smell of a herb or the taste of an oil would remind them of a place or a childhood.

I really loved my customers. They were sometimes challenging, but more often charming, and I was thankful to them for shopping with me because, in addition to the essential social interaction we enjoyed, more income meant more profit, and that meant more buying trips, during which I'd get ever closer to the source of great food. Of the many thousands of people who shopped at Realfood over the years, inevitably I had a few favourites. They were people from many countries and from all walks of life, united in loving the language of food. For them, I'd shop with particular care, knowing which of them especially loved cardoons, perhaps, or for whose birthday unripe peaches in truffle oil (*persechelle* – only ever produced in Piedmont when late frost threatens) would make a special treat.

Among my favourites were Anna Maria and Fabio Rossi. The Rossis, mother and son, divided their time between New York, London (where they kept a gorgeous art gallery) and Tibet. Originally from Turin, the Rossis had a deep love of food, a great sense of chic and a zest for life that I found irresistible. New Years for the Rossis were always spent in London, and in the week before Christmas I would always sell them lentils. Not any lentils, you understand, but Good-luck lentils. Of the seven types of lentil that we offered, it was the tiny green/brown ones from Castelluccio in Umbria that I'd keep for the Rossis. They were a pretty price but had a flavour all of their own: subtle and fine and earthy all at once.

Anna Maria and Fabio would throw a party every New Year's Eve. They'd offer dish after dish of vegetables and *zampone* (stuffed pig's trotter, a speciality of Modena), all accompanied by enormous helpings of Good-luck lentils. These lentils signified good luck and money – each spoonful of tiny 'coins' meant that you'd have more of each in the year to come.

Anna Maria would explain that the good luck came in part from the clear, easy-to-understand flavours of their cooking. Clear, you realize, like our intention and our conscience should be. 'We don't like to confuse our flavours too much,' she said, 'We wouldn't put both garlic and onions in the same dish, or use more than one herb. That would be to muddy the flavour, not to be clear.'

This recipe owes its foundation *sofrito* to the trio of onions, carrots and celery that can also be tasted in Michele Franzolin's recipe for Cod with refried beans (page 78). It is a classic combination that offers a sense of gentle sweet heat to those dishes it flavours, with the celery a memory of the lovage so beloved of ancient Romans.

The dish is presented in its vegetarian version. A richer offering can be made by adding pancetta or *lardo* to the vegetables at the start of the recipe, and replacing the bouillon with chicken stock.

## serves 8

**preparation about 1 hour, plus making the stock**

**1 onion**
**2 carrots**
**3 celery stalks**
**about 3 tablespoons olive oil, plus more to serve**
**500g small lentils**
**4 bay leaves**
**1.5 litres bouillon (made from Swiss vegetable bouillon powder or from stock cubes, or made fresh)**
**salt and black pepper**

♥ Chop the vegetables very small with a mezzaluna or sharp knife. (Food processors tend to tear the fibres of vegetables, and in this case, will cause them to lose too much of their juice.)

♥ Soften the mixture with about 3 tablespoons of oil in a heavy-based pan over a very gentle heat; go slowly and take care not to burn the mixture. A little water added to the pan will help if burning threatens.

♥ Throw in the lentils and the bay leaves, and add enough bouillon to cover the lentils easily. Season to taste.

♥ Bring to the boil and cook, covered, at a simmer for about 45 minutes. Check after 30 minutes, or so – the liquid should be mostly absorbed into the lentils; if the dish is still very wet, cook the last 15 minutes uncovered.

♥ Taste for seasoning and serve warm. Have a little olive oil to hand, for guests to stir into their lentils if they'd like.

# the Egyptian paradox

Egypt is the country that inspired the Sphinx, as well as Wilson, Kepple and Betty, Moses and the Pharaohs, *Ice Cold in Alex* and the Burning Bush. Watered by the north-flowing Nile but defined by desert, Egypt offers myriad paradoxical images that appear at once familiar and alien.

The Egyptian paradox is apparent at all levels. Take the pyramids: 4,500 years ago, Imhotep (right-hand man to King Zoser and later a demi-god himself) was inspired by a mystical vision which offered him the form and technique of building pyramidical structures that would serve as potent repositories for the essential ka (or power) of generations of god-kings. Modern Western man worries over the maths and makes TV about the logistics of their construction; Egyptians, while dependent on the tourists they lure, privately dismiss them as the product of a backward time. This in spite of the fact that Egypt once led the world in architecture, construction, medicine, art and philosophy, yet is now utterly reliant on Western aid.

A total of around seventy pyramids were built in a continuous process during a golden age that lasted a scant 200 years. *Fellahin* peasants were free for half of each year when the Nile flooded, and would have fallen willingly to the exalted work of glorifying their deities in this early example of the production line. Pyramids were prominent in the national consciousness, their shape mirrored everywhere in the Egyptian countryside, from the planes of the mountains that jut sharp-edged into the Gulf of Suez to the lines of the sunbeams that burst through the rare mercy of rain clouds. The elemental symbolism of the pyramids would have been appreciated at all strata of the society that built them, and their erection marked what is arguably the first known example of the state as an organized entity.

Pyramids proclaimed peace and progress and civil service made concrete. In an era when all was yet to be invented, let alone organized, they embodied pure politics, illustrating that the wishes of the people and the will of the state were inseparable. Sheathed as they were in pure-white polished limestone, they attracted and reflected the brilliant light fundamental to sun-cult worship, and provided potent resting places for the immortalized remains and paraphernalia of pharaohs and their families.

The road to the most famous pyramids, at Giza, travels 14 kilometres from the mad bustle of modern Cairo and the journey can take either 20 minutes or three hours, depending on your luck. The soundtrack for the taxi trip is usually the tender melancholy songs of Assala, accented by cadenzas of syrupy strings that echo each sigh of her longing. For much of its length, the road follows the broad green fertile world of the Nile, crossing it eventually to confront random windowless apartment blocks punctuated by fields lush with purslane and *molochiya*, the leaves of which the national dish, a soupy chicken casserole, depends on.

After navigating through lively street markets and past irrigation channels populated by market-ready livestock, the pyramid of Cheops rises without warning through the haze from behind a scrum of souvenir huts. Viewing the three Giza pyramids requires the visitor to do battle with successive waves of urchin trinket vendors and grimy petty officials, all agitating for unearned baksheesh, each utterly shameless in the pursuit of your wallet. There are camel jockeys for whom no starting price is too high (nor sales pitch too repetitive), and leery unofficial guides with the charm and tenacity of head lice, whose insistent demands for attention nearly ruin any chance of enjoying the compelling power of the pyramids.

However, in spite of our familiarity with their image and no matter how exasperating the attentions of the people who infest them, the pyramids still exert a pull so strong as to be surprising and genuinely awe-inspiring. We are prepared for their bulk, but the impression that one retains is not simply of size or scale, but of unforgotten wonder. The three dimensions and perfect planes of their triangular silhouette are intensely uplifting – there is vicarious pride to be taken in appreciating that the elevation of such elemental forms was a human achievement.

Returning to the city centre is a matter of adding to the astonishing and constant road congestion. Cairo sprawls and boils with nearly 19 million inhabitants who incinerate their waste in the streets and burn their environmental bridges in an unplanned, unregulated building spree. In physiological terms, Cairo is a patient for whom surgery would surely prove too dangerous and too late. In the manner of a cholesterol that clogs arteries, the traffic lurches or oozes or simply stops altogether, giving the city the *mien* of a wheezing, honking old man.

In the 14th century, Islamic Cairo, centred on the Khan-e-Khalili bazaar, was among the wonders of the world, thought by the historian Ibn Khaldoun to be 'the metropolis of the universe, the garden of the world, the nest of the human species...'

As the only great Arab capital to have survived intact (Cordoba and Baghdad both fell), Islamic Cairo retains an authentically medieval atmosphere, with an all-pervading sense of reality and mystery that is quite unburdened by any Hollywood fantasy. Beshawled and turbaned shoppers and hawkers compete for space with donkeys and barrows in narrow alleys overhung by balconies and bunting. The city is inhabited by powerful smells and a deeply religious population for whom the countless crowded minarets are their only skyscrapers. Five times a day, the timeless quality of Islamic Cairo's belief is buttressed by the amplified calls to prayer that emanate and vibrate from all around, suffusing the fabric of the city and the hearts of its people with their poetry and devotion.

Tourists are welcomed as another crop to be bought, sold and consumed, but the sensibility of Islamic Cairo is more to do with daily survival and promulgation of the faith than with monument restoration or destination marketing. The result is an unexpurgated, unsanitized version of Ibn Khaldoun's city, little changed by modern times, an exciting, enervating reflection of the traditions and imperfections of another age.

West of the Islamic city lies Downtown, bordered on one side by the Nile. The business and administrative heart of the country is home also to the Egyptian Museum, a rambling warehouse full of pharaonic treasure where the jumble of rooms, dusty cabinets and inadequate signing and lighting fails to dim the luminous quality of the artefacts on display. Guides point torches at the salient features of sculptures, Canon-wielding tourists, visiting historians and sketching students stumble between exhibits, visibly inspired and impressed by such lively relics of a long-dead era.

Lacquered funeral caskets the size of small bungalows fit inside each other in the manner of Russian dolls, intricately carved alabaster thrones and delicate golden pony-traps compete for our attention with mummified monkeys and 4,000-year-old bread rolls.

In one of the rooms, the antimonied eyes of the statues appear alive and possessed of some vital, inordinate gnosis; a side gallery showcases gorgeous, lustrous, scintillating jewellery of astonishingly accomplished art and craft. The star attraction of the museum and Egypt's modern mascot is Tutankhamun. Now returned home after his triumphant 1970s World Tour, Tutankhamun has a large room to himself, filled with the rich golden trappings of his power. His photogenic androgynous features continue to cast their spell on all who gaze upon him; his loyal subjects now include postcard manufacturers and leisure-suited holidaymakers.

What King Tut would have made of contemporary Cairo is debatable. Stepping from the museum of ancient glories into the modern midden of Midan-el-Tahir, the city's main square, the impression gained is of epochs colliding, the older one winning. Cairo has motor cars in abundance, but driven sheep and donkey-drawn carts are commonplace. The car, too, illustrates the Cairo paradox, with entire districts given over to auto accessories – gleaming alloy wheels, air-con kits and so on – yet the majority of drivers choose to conduct their snail-pace after-dark driving without headlights, relying instead on randomly repeated blasts of their horns. Traffic lights, though invariably attended by at least a pair of uniformed police, are, for the most part, ignored; busy intersections therefore take half an hour to negotiate in peak periods.

There are thousands of raffish taxis, each equipped with a broken meter, bald tyres and a rally champion behind the wheel. Agreeing a tariff takes time and patience out of all proportion to the length of the journey. Depending on the fee agreed and the driver's level of contentment with it, the trip may take minutes or hours, and possibly years off your life.

Better by far is to travel by the measured throb of a river bus, or to tack and eddy downriver on a felucca. The Nile is the heart, lungs, liver and blood of the nation: 93 per cent of Egyptians live within a mile of its banks. The unremitting nature of Cairo is relieved by the broad Nile, from where the city's water supply is drawn and into which it discharges its waste. The river flows serene, deep green and slow through the west of town, where foreign embassies and international hotels straddle its banks and those of its islands.

Everywhere there is food. Next to the egg sellers, pigeons destined for stuffing and grilling brood silently by the roadside, crammed into bamboo cages, on top of which sit scrawny, gamey turkeys displaying fanned tail-feathers. Vegetable merchants sit cross-legged, protected from shrieking, bargaining customers behind circled forts of green onions. Fat fruiterers, their stalls piled high with dates and bananas, park themselves outside grocery stores that boast baskets of *molochiya* and ladder-high stacks of tinned and jarred preserves. Walls washed sea-blue or *haj*-green denote the slaughterers' shops, with calves' feet proudly displayed and tripe hanging from a ceiling hook. Butchers sharing *sheesha* pipes with their customers look on while scruffy kids with eyes of molten cocoa cajole and blackmail pens and baksheesh out of pink tourists, fresh meat on their block. 'How much rich are you?' they chorus, a statement as much as a question.

The moderately wealthy eat out in restaurants. During Ramadan and national holidays, restaurants spill out on to the streets, when the exuberant chatter of table melds with the ululating rhythms of *tabla* and *uid* and the throb of belly-dance *baladi* beat. Once-ritzy joints that were fashionable pre-Nasser, such as the sedate Alfi Bey, serve piles of sour flat breads and meltingly soft koftas and grilled half-chickens, thoughtfully providing boxes of tissues on each table for greasy fingers.

Also in Downtown, among the bureaux de change and the 1970s-fasciaed clothes shops with names like 'Moderne' and 'I Like It!' is Felfela Alaa el Din, home to the best *ta'amia* (falafel) in Cairo, and perhaps the best anywhere. The *ta'amia* are made from stridently spiced crushed white broad beans, moulded into patties the size of a large walnut, and quickly deep-fried in fresh oil. When their crisp dark shells split to reveal a temptingly light, still-steaming filling, Felfela's falafel sharpen the most jaded appetite and incite excesses in even the most timid of eaters.

The Citadel commands the medieval tenements of Islamic Cairo. Down the meanest of streets and on the corner that defines the limits of the old city is Aboo

Ramy. This sprawling restaurant sits opposite what was the old open-air abattoir, and has grown huge over the years. A favourite with celebrities and locals alike, diners sit just out of the gutter in a restaurant that caters for up to 500. Tables and chairs are rude and the service, though eccentric (waiters sporting black bin-bags with holes cut out for head and arms), is charming and efficient, a paean to perpetual motion as trays of starters – cumin-spiked mixed salad, tahini paste, sesame aubergine *baba ghanouj*, salty yoghurt, aggressive pickles (local whisky, they call them) – are hurried by at head height. Twisty sausages, slick grilled lambs' intestines stuffed with offal, and juicy lamb chops are served with double-minced *koftas* so light that they render every last mouthful a vague savoury memory; all

are displayed on huge mounds of chopped parsley and accompanied by teetering stacks of rough, puffed-up wholemeal bread. A pre-adolescent girl is encouraged to stand on a chair; she dances coquettish arabesques to an oriental beat box and the air fills with the sound of clapping and laughter.

Old Cairo also has numerous *koushary* shops. *Koushary* is street food, working food and a great leveller. Brightly lit window displays of man-sized mounds of rice, of chickpeas and spicy tomato sauce tempt passers-by from all walks of life to a fuel stop. The *koushary* version of rice, where it is cooked with macaroni, confuses Western sensibilities by mixing two starches in the same dish, but is a satisfying contrast of tastes and textures. Too much *koushary* may make you walk like an Egyptian, but no dish better illustrates the Egyptian paradox, where pasta is cooked with rice, where the future is behind them and the past continues to happen.

This recipe is a (somewhat refined) version of the rice served in *koushary* shops. It demonstrates rice to be the easy, tasty convenience food that it is for half the world.

# Egyptian rice with vermicelli

serves 4

**preparation 40 minutes, plus 15 minutes resting**

**500g basmati rice**
**light vegetable oil, for frying**
**1 nest of vermicelli**
**sea salt**

*Alfi Bey*
*3 Sharia al Alfi, 771 888*
*Felfela Alaa el Din*
*15 Sharia Hoda Sharawi, 392 2833*
*Aboo Ramy*
*Zein el Abidin (no number)*

♥ Put the rice in a measuring jug to assess its volume. Tip out and measure 1½ times that volume of water.

♥ In a heavy pan (which has a tight-fitting lid) over a high heat, heat the oil and stir in the vermicelli well. It will brown in seconds.

♥ As soon as it does, throw in the rice and stir for a minute, until every grain has a coating of oil.

♥ Add the measured water and bring to the boil. Stir in salt to taste and cover firmly. Reduce the heat to very low and cook, undisturbed, for about 20 minutes, until tender but still with a bite (exact time will vary slightly, depending on age and quality of the rice).

♥ Take off the heat and fork through it to separate the grains further. Allow the rice to rest, covered again, for about 15 minutes.

♥ Serve with Onion-smothered chicken with sharp lemon and hamine eggs (page 82) or No-salt massaged shoulder of lamb (page 66).

# Fail-safe tomato sauce

Inspired by the doyenne of Italian food writers, Marcella Hazan, this sauce is tasty, easy and economical! It's worth making in bigger quantities as it keeps for up to 4 days in a refrigerator.

serves 6

**preparation 1 hour**

**1.5 kg tomatoes, skinned, cored, and roughly chopped (or tinned)**
**1 large onion, cut in half**
**250g unsalted butter**
**sea salt to taste**
**1 tablespoon sugar (if using early or not-quite-ripe tomatoes)**

♥ Place all the ingredients in a heavy pan over a low heat.

♥ After about 10 minutes, start to crush the tomatoes against the side of the pan with a wooden spoon. Repeat every 10 minutes or so, leaving the pan uncovered. After 40 minutes or so, you'll have a thick sauce – it's ready when a film of fat rises to the top.

♥ Remove the onion (and keep it – it's delicious chopped into salads or stews), taste and adjust the seasoning.

♥ Our kids love, love, love this sauce, but will only eat it if it has been sieved or strained or blitzed with an electric wand.

# Minoo's celery khoresh

A *khoresh* is Persian stew, to be served with basmati rice. Many *khoreshta* have involved, complicated recipes, but this one, given by my cousin Minoo Sueke (whose family, the Ghodsians, now live in Los Angeles), is easy and quick. Its proper name is *Khorest e Karafs*.

## serves 4

**preparation about 1 hour**

2 large onions, thinly sliced
2 garlic cloves, finely chopped
½ teaspoon ground turmeric
2 large celery stalks, cut into 2cm pieces, the leaves finely chopped
sea salt and freshly ground black pepper
about 3 tablespoons olive oil
1 cup of finely chopped fresh parsley
a kettleful of boiling water
225g tin of chopped tomatoes
1 cup of crushed dried mint
juice of 2–3 lemons

♥ Place the onions and garlic in a 25cm saucepan, sprinkle with turmeric and place the celery (not the leaves) on top. Add salt and pepper, and sprinkle with the oil.
♥ Cover the pan and set it over a low-to-medium heat for 10 minutes.
♥ Stir well, add the celery leaves and parsley, and cover again.
♥ After 2 or 3 minutes, at any rate before the celery burns, cover the contents with boiling water.
♥ Cover and cook until the celery is tender but still a little crunchy.
♥ Add the tomatoes and dried mint to the pan, season with more salt and pepper (if needed), and add lemon juice to taste. The *khoresh* should be quite tart, as a counterpoint to the plain rice.
♥ Simmer, uncovered, for 20 minutes, adding a little more water should the mixture start to stick.

For a chicken version, cut 4 skinless chicken breast fillets into large chunks and colour these lightly in a little oil. Add 2 extra finely chopped garlic cloves, stir well, then add the turmeric, seasoning and oil as above. Stir-fry for 10 minutes, adding a little water if the garlic should start to catch. Meanwhile, cook the celery with the onions, garlic, parsley and some seasoning only as above. Add the chicken, etc., to the pan of celery after the tomatoes, mint and lemon juice.

# kalti barsh or kulti buchsh

This boil-in-the-bag dish is straight out of the Bukharan repertoire, in which rice is a staple, the cuisine being influenced by the neighbouring countries of Russia, Iran and Afghanistan. Samarkand before the Bolsheviks was a multicultural place, where Armenians, Jews, Slavs, Caucasians, Persians and Pathans came together to trade the silk and spices borne by camel caravans through its centre.

*Kalti barsh* was a dish traditional to the Jews of Samarkand, and every bride would have a boiling bag as part of her dowry. Today, use a punctured roasting bag for this dish, or make up a bag of pure cotton or linen for the sheer pleasure of it. Alternatively, increase the recipe quantities and make a party dish in a pillowcase!

serves 6

**preparation about 2 hours**

225g chicken livers
350g basmati rice
225g minced beef
a bunch of fresh coriander, coarsely chopped
225g frozen spinach, defrosted
2 tablespoons chopped fresh dill
1 chicken stock cube
2 tablespoons sunflower oil
3 tablespoons boiling water, plus more for the cooking
salt and pepper

♥ Place the chicken livers in a saucepan and cover with cold water. Bring to the boil, then remove from the heat and drain. Rinse the livers and chop them.

♥ In a large bowl, combine the chopped livers with all the ingredients and mix together well. Carefully spoon everything into the cotton or a roasting bag, or a pillowcase. Knot the bag well, allowing some space for the rice to swell. If using a roasting bag, pierce it here and there on both sides.

♥ Place in a pan and cover with boiling water, bring back to the boil, then reduce the heat and simmer very gently for 1½ hours, checking every so often to make sure that the bag is completely covered with water.

♥ Serve on a large platter, taking care not to burn your hands

# 15-minute tarte tatin with Calvados

The locals know it as 'The End of the World'. La Grand Vey is less than a village, more than a hamlet, just along the coast from Omaha Beach in Normandy. It was from here that William the Conqueror fled over the sands to evade his enemies. When the tide goes is out, the beach at Le Grand Vey stretches all the way to distant Isigny, home of the world's best crème fraîche and Camembert cheeses.

In 1999, the local grocery store, Chez Roger, was bought by top Norman chef Joel Meslin, as a place to play in when he retires. The store has become a 30-cover restaurant, and a room upstairs has been turned into a private room for 20, with distant views out to sea. 'This is not so much *restauration*,' insists Joel, 'but is more like *chez soi*.' He's right – guests are just as likely to be asked to wash up their dishes as they are to be offered the run of the bar, stocked full as it is with local Calvados.

Joel is a farmer's son who started work aged 14 as a roof thatcher. He has grown into a great bear of a man, burly and big, with a thatch of blond hair. In the tiny kitchen, his bulk seems to vanish – he dances around on the balls of his feet, moving swiftly and gracefully between sink and work surface. Joel works as only a cook at the top of his *métier* is able: concentrated yet relaxed, with a fierce pride in the quality of his ingredients.

This is his *tarte tatin*, to be served warm after a long and happy meal. When making and eating it, do think of Norman star-sparkly nights, the moon high over Le Grand Vey, and remember Joel Meslin's maxim, that the best place to be is where '*vous*' becomes '*tu*'.

serves 6

**preparation 45 minutes**

4 dessert apples, peeled, cored
and cut into eighths
50g butter
50g granulated sugar
about 4 tablespoons Calvados
500g shop-bought puff pastry,
defrosted
crème fraîche, to serve

♥ Preheat the oven to 220°C.

♥ Fry the apples in the butter over a medium heat in a shallow frying or *tarte tatin* pan, adding the sugar early and stirring well.

♥ Add as much Calvados as you like and cook for a minute or so, then remove from the heat. Layer the apple pieces in the pan.

♥ Roll out the pastry and place it on top of the apples, so that it slightly overlaps the pan. Trim to the edge of the pan.

♥ Prick the pastry all over with a fork and bake for 20 minutes.

♥ Remove from the oven and let settle for 5 minutes before turning out.

♥ Serve warm (reheat in the pan if needed) with crème fraîche.

# grilled fresh pineapple and jammy figs

serves 4

**preparation about 30
minutes**

1 juicy medium-sized pineapple
vegetable oil, for greasing
3 fresh figs, sliced in half lengthwise
Greek yoghurt or crème fraîche, to serve
aromatic runny honey, such as
chestnut, to serve

♥ Peel the pineapple and cut it into 1cm slices. Heat a very lightly oiled griddle pan over a low-to-medium heat and grill the pineapple slices until their natural juices start to caramelize, then turn them over and cook the other side.

♥ Place the figs cut side down on the grill. Cook until the juices start to bubble and smell caramelized.

♥ Serve the fruits with Greek yoghurt or crème fraîche, and perhaps a spoonful or two of aromatic runny honey.

# pomegranate jelly with cream

In the Near and Middle East, newlyweds are given the gift of a pomegranate tree to bring good luck. Its shade offers succour, its fruit (not unlike marriage!) is both sweet and sharp, and its many seeds symbolize fertility. This set jelly showcases the pomegranate's garnet brightness and grenadine flavour. If fresh pomegranates aren't available, buy pomegranate molasses and dilute in 7 parts of water to approximate the fresh juice.

**makes around 750ml (about 4 good servings)**

**preparation about 20 minutes, plus at least 5½ hours' chilling**

**1 small and 1 large pomegranate
about 100ml grenadine syrup
juice of 1 small lemon
5 sheets of gelatine, soaked according to the instructions on the pack
pouring cream, to serve**

♥ Remove the seeds from the small pomegranate. Squeeze the juice from the large pomegranate. (The most reckless way to squeeze a pomegranate is to stab it all over with a sharp knife, then to roll it under your heavy palm on a board, catching the flowing juices.)

♥ Measure the juice and add an equal quantity of water and an equal quantity of grenadine syrup, then strain in the lemon juice.

♥ Heat the gelatine in a pan with a quarter of all the liquid mixture until it dissolves.

♥ Add to the rest of the liquid, pour into a big bowl and chill for 1½ hours.

♥ Then stir in the seeds from the small pomegranate, reserving a few of them for decoration.

♥ Pour the liquid into one large or several small moulds, then chill for at least 4 hours.

♥ Serve dressed with the reserved seeds and a whisper of white cream around each serving. Pretty and delicious!

# chapter five
## eating with a lover

Cooking food for someone you fancy does not always have to be a fancy affair. In my experience, grandstand gourmandizing can result in soufflés that refuse to rise to the occasion, and, in addition, you run the risk of making yourself into an olfactory turnoff.

I once wrote a magazine article suggesting that the food we eat actually affects the way our bodies smell. Perfectly straightforward, you might say. Stands to reason, I might agree – somewhere during the digestive process supper becomes sweat. There are sweat glands in abundance under the armpits and in the jockey area, and dotted liberally all over the body, the back of the neck being particularly perspiration-prolific, apparently. As it's unlikely that the entire skin surface could be deodorized, I concluded that, in addition to the latest fashion, super-smart fragrance and a dishy smile, we're also wearing *eau de diner*. There was outrage – perfect strangers accosted me in the streets. 'Are ye trying to tell me that I smell like a meat pie?' demanded one particularly angry Scotsman. (He did.) And so on for weeks and weeks.

The Western taboo that I'd unwittingly touched upon was that it is considered uncivilized to smell like you. You can smell like flowers, or bananas, or spice. You can even smell like Calvin Klein wants you to (although, until he's willing to smell like I want him to, I'm not playing, thank you, Calvin). Anyway, the conceit of the piece was that one should, wherever possible, serve food that will leave a good smell on the skin. We know how garlic so quickly migrates to the breath and the sweat, but what of other foods? My information suggested, among other findings, that the scent of vanilla on female sweat arouses strong filial feelings in men, as vanilla smells very similar to breast milk. Oh, and that eating pineapple caused the seed to taste sweet. The man from Del Monte, he say... All of which adds new emphasis to the idea 'Love me, love my food', albeit with the rider attached, 'Eat my food, eat me.'

The extension of which takes us into more wholesome territory – the notion of making an offering of yourself to your lover or your God. Such surrender, such selflessness, says. 'Take me – I am your gift'. The corollary of which is that we should all make ourselves good food for God.

In his *Conversations with God*, Neale David Acheson has life explained to him thus: 'The heart is the seat of the soul. Speaking [and cooking, I would definitely say!] from the heart kindles that fire in others. Fire spreads: there is nothing more catching than Love!' So, if ever you needed it on a plate, here it is: don't just make lunch – make love!

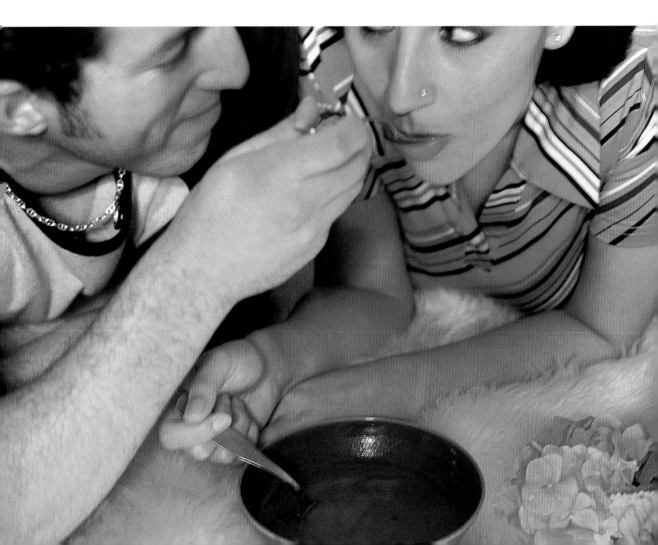

# consummation consommé

Why consummation? This is a lucky soup, designed to bring a relationship to fruition. It is a classic consommé, performed without the fuss of clarifying it (cooking with egg white, then filtering until absolutely clear), but made fragrant with dried wild mushrooms, then finished with some good wine. Make this soup with care, understanding what you might be getting yourself into as a result.

makes 5 litres (and, without the wine, a wonderful stock which freezes well)

**preparation about 4½ hours**

2kg lean beef, cut into rough chunks
1.5kg bone-in beef shank, sawn into chunks by your butcher, or lean stewing beef, cut into chunks
coarse salt
4 carrots, peeled
4 leeks, trimmed and tied together
2 celery stalks, tied together with 1 bay leaf between them
1 medium-sized onion, stuck with 2 cloves
2 garlic cloves
20g dried porcini
a sprig of thyme
a bottle of good red wine
a little very finely chopped parsley, for garnish

♥ Put the meat in a large stockpot with 7 litres of water and bring to the boil. Skim off the scum, then season with salt.

♥ Add the rest of the ingredients, except the wine and parsley, and simmer very, very slowly for 4 hours.

♥ Remove the meat and drain the stock very carefully. Pat the top of the stock with kitchen towel to remove any traces of fat. (If you have time, leave it to cool overnight, then skim off all the white fat that has risen to the top.)

♥ Reheat the stock and, just before serving, pour half a glass of wine into each bowl. Serve garnished with the merest sprinkling of parsley.

# white asparagus wrapped in ham

serves 2

**preparation 10–15 minutes**

7 (or more) big thick spears of white asparagus (3 each and one to share)
1 lemon
freshly ground sea salt and coarsely ground black pepper
a little olive oil
7 (or more) perfect slices of wafer thin cured ham, such as *jamón de Jabugo, prosciutto di Parma* or *jambon de Bayonne*

♥ Peel the thick ends of the asparagus with a vegetable peeler until they taper suggestively.

♥ Boil the asparagus in lightly salted water with the juice of half a lemon until just tender, about 5 minutes.

♥ Rub the flimsiest film of olive oil over one side of each slice of ham, then dust a little coarse black pepper over it. Roll the ham slice around a spear of asparagus, oiled side inwards.

♥ Serve with the merest sprinkle of lemon juice, the suggestion of a smile playing around the corners of your pretty mouth.

# deda's puri with Georgian wine

Georgia is a young republic with an ancient history. Sharing frontiers with her Chechniyan, Dagestani and Azerbaijani neighbours, and bordered by Russia to the north and Turkey and Armenia to the south, Georgia has one foot in the East of the Silk Road and the other in the West of the busy shipping lanes of the Black Sea. Her head is crowned by the thickly wooded mass of the Caucasus mountains, whose snow-capped peaks water the fertile valleys of her heart. And it is the rich soil of these valleys that grows the wheat from which *deda's puri* is made. *Deda's puri* (mother's dough) is inseparable from the Georgian national consciousness. To a nation raised on feasting, no meal is complete without mother's bread, the background against which all food and wine is tasted.

Georgian breads come in all shapes – long ovals with 'handles' at each end, rough circles with a hole in the middle, rectangles into the centres of which are broken eggs and are baked salty cheeses. In Tibilisi, the capital, ramshackle bakeries offer chewy loaves baked over wood fires; village and street markets all over the country feature stalls piled high with bread: emeretian (*emeruli*), with cows' cheese, adjarian (*acharuli*) with goats' cheese and buttered eggs. The Jews of Georgia have contributed *lobiani* – bread baked with red beans (and no dairy products to contravene *kashrut*) – and there are spinach breads and (a gift from the Russians) potato bread.

Bread is joined in the national psyche by wine. Georgia's heart beats with a pride born from the knowledge that she is the oldest wine-making nation in the world. The roots of her viticulture stretch back to between 7000 and 5000 BC, when Caucasian man discovered that wild grape juice turned into happy juice when it was left buried through the winter in a shallow pit. This knowledge was nourished by experience, and from 4000 BC Georgians were cultivating grapes and burying clay vessels, *kvevri*, storing their wine ready for serving at perfect ground temperature.

When it came to expressing their unique language in written form, Georgians used the shapes of the vine to provide the sinuous, flowing alphabet that remains in use today. To European ears, spoken Georgian contains very few recognizable words, with the grand exception of *ghvino*, or wine, the pronunciation of which was disseminated from here to the rest of the world by the Phoenicians and the Greeks.

This love affair with the grape was given further encouragement by the arrival of St Nino in the 4th century. Fleeing Roman persecution in Cappadocia, in what is now central Anatolia, and bearing a cross made of vine wood and bound with her own hair, St Nino was swept up in the warm embrace of the Georgians, who became early converts to Christianity. Thus cross and vine became inextricably linked, and perhaps interchangeable symbols, in the Georgian psyche, and the advent of the new faith served to sanction the vinous practices of the old.

Not all visitors, however, were welcomed as warmly as St Nino. Among the invaders who have tested the Georgians' legendary hospitality were the Ottomans, who stuffed their harems full of the shapely, pale-skinned, dark-eyed Circassian girls. Recent history witnessed the arrival of the Soviets, whose futile attempts at controlling this free-living race must have frustrated many a Motherland functionary. The legacy of the great Soviet experiment – which ended with Georgian liberation in 1992 – is an appallingly messy infrastructure, although this burden has done nothing to dim the stupendously ironic Georgian sense of humour, which turns on self-deprecation and straight-faced stabs at authority figures.

When it comes to wine-making, though, Georgia is blessed. Extremes of weather are unusual: summers tend to be sunny, and winters mild and frost-free. Natural springs abound, and the Caucasian mountain streams drain mineral-rich water into the valleys. Together with luscious tomatoes, the sweetest white and red cherries, and any amount of wild mulberries, the Kakheti region in the east, which is one of Georgia's five main wine regions, also produces what might be among the world's finest grapes. Although there are nearly 500 to choose from, only 38 varieties of grape are officially grown for commercial viticulture in Georgia.

Like most of his neighbours in the Napareuli area of Kakheti, Andrea, a wise 76-year-old with compassionate blue eyes and grey moustache, grows Rkatsiteli grapes for white wine and Saperavi for red, all of which are destined for the winery of the Georgian Wine and Spirit Company (GWS).

When Georgia was producing three-quarters of all wine drunk in the Soviet Union, some 25 decilitres a year of indifferent plonk were churned out to service a guaranteed, subsidized market intent on taking a mental holiday from Communism by way of heavy drinking. Today, with some sensitive investment from French drinks company Pernod Ricard, the sure hand of GWS chief wine-maker Tamaz Kandelaki and the youthful energy of flying Australian wizard David Nelson are converting Andrea's grapes into limited-edition, astonishing red and white wines of unusual character.

Wines such as Old Tibilisi and the rich, honey-coloured Tamada, both made with Rkatsiteli grapes, marry the tradition of the Old World with the verve of the New. The reds tend towards the tobacco or spice styles so loved by the Californians, with the well-balanced Saperavi deserving particular praise. Most impressive, perhaps, are the semi-sweet wines. These shapely beauties, such as the red Pirosmani and the white Tvishi, made with Tsolikauri grapes, manage to avoid the sticky oiliness of many a dessert wine, delivering instead an enchanting mouthful of complex, developing flavours. Pirosmani straddles a meal with ease, being equally at home as a chilled aperitif and with a dessert of fresh cherries and apricots.

Some of the wine made from Andrea's grapes will be ceremoniously returned to the ground. Just like his forefathers, Andrea has a consecrated place, a *marani*, dug out under his house, where he buries clay *kvevri*, and the wine matures courtesy of the cooling properties of underground streams. When filled with the juice of the harvest, the *kvevris* are topped with a wooden lid and then covered and sealed with earth.

Gathering his closest family around him, and wearing a black felt helmet, the family patriarch presides over the emotional moment when a *kvevri*'s lid is removed. Intoning a toast of thanks and praise, he scoops a shallow earthenware bowl into the surprised liquid, and with the salutation '*Galmajous!*' drinks it down in one. As more bowls are filled, the menfolk chant the powerfully plangent song '*Mravalzhamier*', 'Many Years of Life,' in millennia-old polyphonic harmonies. Wiping away unembarrassed tears, the men then fill plastic jerry cans to be borne triumphantly to the feast.

If Georgia's spirit is her grape, then her body is the feast, where all life is celebrated and thanks are offered to St Nino and all Nature's spirits. Georgians feast regularly, and Andrea's ancestors have been feasting in the same secluded glade since the 6th century, when a priest named Abraham built a stone chapel to shelter his flock from invading Persians.

A long wooden table for 30, set next to a rushing river, groans under the banquet. Aubergines with walnuts and wild garlic sit next to piles of purple basil, green tarragon and flushed pink radishes. Salty cheeses and wild mushroom salads with dill-heavy green beans complement piles of *deda's puri*. Platters of fat sausages and bowls of corn-yellow chicken legs are passed around, and a fire of crackling vine cuttings is on the go. Chunks of seasoned lamb and marinated suckling pig are kebabed on branches of green beech and Andrea is elected *tamada*, or toastmaster.

Baskets of cherries and plums are brought out, and the *tamada* hums the first few bars of a melody. With hearts full of the Georgian grape, the feasters link arms. Looking into each other's eyes, they praise the moment when breath mingles with spirit and life is lived to the full. '*Galmajous!*' It is in the exuberant, affectionate toast of the Georgian feast that you should offer this bread, accompanied (of course!) by great draughts of wine, to your lover. The recipe is adapted from Julianne Margvelashvili's *The Classic Cuisine of Soviet Georgia* and is delicious by itself or with cheese – with a bottle of Georgian wine, of course!

## makes 6 small loaves

**preparation about 1
hour, plus standing**

¼ **cup of just-boiled water**
¼ **teaspoon sugar**
**1 packet (15g) of dried yeast**
¾ **cup of lukewarm water**
**1 teaspoon salt**
2¾ **cups of unbleached plain flour,
plus more for dusting**
**light vegetable oil**

♥ Put the just-boiled water in a small bowl and dissolve the sugar in it, then the yeast. Let the mixture stand in a warm place for about 10 minutes, until it bubbles and doubles in volume.

♥ Pour the mixture into a large bowl and stir in the lukewarm water, salt and flour. Mix well until a dough is formed.

♥ Turn out on to a floured board and knead for 10–15 minutes, by which time the dough should become smooth and elastic.

♥ Warm and lightly oil the large bowl and place the dough in it. Turn the dough over a few times to coat it in oil. Cover with a clean tea towel and let stand in a warm place until doubled in bulk.

♥ Meanwhile, preheat the oven as hot as it will go (ideally 230°C).

♥ Punch down the dough a couple of times, then divide into 6. With floured hands, gently pat each piece into a circle about 1cm thick. Place on a lightly greased baking sheet and make a hole all the way through the centre of each with your finger.

♥ Cook in the top third of the oven for 10–12 minutes, and serve immediately.

**Aquarius, 21 January - 19 February**

**Pisces, 20 February - 20 March**

**Aries, 21 March - 20 April**

**Taurus, 21 April - 21 May**

**Gemini, 22 May - 20 June**

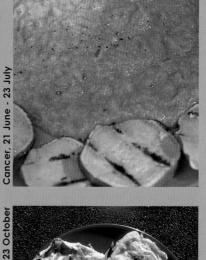

**Cancer, 21 June - 23 July**

**Leo, 24 July - 23 August**

**Virgo, 24 August - 22 September**

**Libra, 23 September - 23 October**

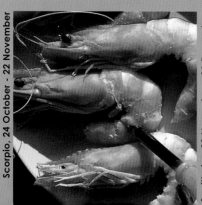

**Scorpio, 24 October - 22 November**

**Sagittarius, 23 November - 20 December**

**Capricorn, 21 December - 20 January**

# signs of the zodiac mezze

In Petronius's *Satyricon*, written around the time of the Emperor Nero, there appears a character called Trimalchio. Trimalchio was the progenitor of F. Scott Fitzgerald's Gatsby. His equivalent today would be someone like Donald Trump, only without the good looks, charm and taste.

Trimalchio was a freed slave who, by shrewd dealing, amassed a fortune that allowed him to indulge in all manner of gaudy excess, from purple and scarlet robes ('with tassels and fringes dingle-dangle') to feasts so vulgar and lavish that his guests sought finally to escape his boorish hospitality. Flashy feast dishes, such as dormice seasoned with honey and poppies or peahens' eggs stuffed with *beccaficos* (fig-peckers) in peppered yolk, were served at Trimalchio's table.

He also offered the clever conceit of signs of the zodiac *fercula* (prepared dishes), recipes for which are given in the recipe book of Roman food writer Apicius. These recipes are not reproduced here, as sterile sow's womb (Virgo), or cakes stuffed with live thrushes (Libra) are perhaps not the must-eat items that they used to be. However, the notion of sun-sign dishes that may prove to be as compatible as the lovers themselves is a delicious one: there may be a certain chemistry between you, but do your dishes mix?

## Aquarius – herring in gin with celery and juniper

Aquarians are both intelligent and practical; at the same time, they make thoughtful and impressive theorists.

**preparation 10 minutes, at least 1 hour in advance**

4 rollmop herrings, skewers removed
4 juniper berries, bruised
200ml gin
juice of ½ lemon
4 pert, fresh celery stalks, about 12cm long

♥ Put the rollmops and juniper in a bowl and add half the gin.

♥ In a wide glass, mix the lemon juice with the rest of the gin.

♥ Fold 2 sheets of kitchen roll several times and submerge in the glass.

♥ Slice off the very bottom of each celery stalk, and stand on the kitchen towel in the glass of gin so they are able to drink the gin by capillary action.

♥ Leave rollmops and celery in the fridge for at least an hour, or overnight.

♥ To serve: wind a rollmop around each celery stalk, and skewer through with a cocktail stick. Souse in whatever liquid is left and serve cold.

# Pisces – soda-siphon prawns

Forthright, subtle and winning, Pisceans understand how to meld.

This recipe was inspired by Ferran Adria of the El Bulli Restaurant, north of Barcelona. Ferran *is* the avant-garde of food, and he delights in confounding established culinary lore. He developed a zabaglione flavoured with crab, which he froths with the aid of a special wide-apertured soda siphon. Here I mimic the results by beating the egg whites, but you could make the mixture even more frothy using an aerolat – one of those portable cappuccino frothers.

**preparation 25 minutes**

1 tablespoon olive oil
1 garlic clove, very finely chopped
100g cooked peeled prawns or shrimp
sea salt
a pinch of saffron
2 teaspoons boiling water
white of 1 egg
200ml bio yoghurt
4 perfect crisp lettuce leaves, to serve
a few cooked prawns in the shell, to garnish
lemon zest, to garnish

♥ Heat the oil in a small saucepan until warm, but not hot. Add the garlic and cook gently until the aroma rises. Remove the garlic before it colours and reserve.

♥ Heat the cooked prawns or shrimp through in the garlic-infused oil and add salt to taste.

♥ Soak the saffron in the boiling water and steep for 5 minutes.

♥ Meanwhile, beat the egg white to soft peaks. Fold the egg white into the yoghurt, then add the saffron and its soaking water.

♥ Amalgamate the yoghurt with the prawns and the reserved garlic and blitz in a food processor briefly until reasonably smooth.

♥ Taste and adjust the seasoning if necessary.

♥ Shake well and spoon or pour the mixture into the lettuce leaves, letting it flow into and fill the ridges and valleys of the lettuce in a trail of froth, like bubbles from a fish's mouth.

♥ Garnish with the prawns in the shell and lemon zest. Serve lightly chilled.

# Aries – lamb's lettuce salad, confit shallots, lemon mint olives, golden almonds

Champions of the challenge, Aries are strong, steadfast and stubbornly loyal. Their capacity for deep emotion is unbounded.

**preparation 25 minutes (plus the olives)**

2 banana shallots or 1 medium onion, very thinly sliced
½ small wine glass of olive oil

♥ Cook the shallots or onions in the oil over a moderate heat. The idea is to soften them and bring out their sweetness, not to colour them. Give them a couple of turns of the peppermill while they cook. (Tip: to slow down the cooking time and to add depth of flavour, add a couple of tablespoons of water or vegetable stock once the oil has been absorbed, then cook until this liquid too is

**sea salt and pepper**
**50g flaked almonds**
**100g lamb's lettuce (mâche)**
**40-day Lemon Mint Olives (page 39)**

subsumed into the sweet, soft shallots or onions.)

♥ In a dry frying pan, toast the almonds with a sprinkle of good fine sea salt or Maldon crystals. Once golden, allow to cool to a crisp.

♥ Mix the lamb's lettuce, olives, shallots or onions and almonds together. No further dressing should be needed, as this may cause the lamb's lettuce to become soggy. Serve at room temperature.

## Taurus – bresaola horns with cream cheese dressing, walnuts and chives

With a taste for fine things, Taureans are excellent connoisseurs. Strong, with huge reserves of passion, they make great friends!

**preparation 15 minutes**

**150g soft cream cheese (cow or goat)**
**cayenne pepper**
**25g toasted walnuts, roughly chopped**
**a little olive oil**
**6 very thin slices of bresaola**
**1 chive stalk**
**cherry tomatoes, to garnish, if you like**

♥ Mash the cream cheese with a fork, working in the tiniest hint of cayenne – attempt to achieve the impression of slightly flushed skin. Mix in the walnuts.

♥ Rub a very thin film of olive oil on one side of each slice of bresaola. This will keep it malleable and soft.

♥ Place a heaped teaspoon or so of the blushing cheese towards the top of each slice of bresaola, then roll into a cornet, the nutty cheese peeping coyly from the top.

♥ With a pair of scissors, snip some tiny ribbons of chives over the cheese. (Chives should be treated with caution if onion breath is to be avoided. In this dish, the chives should hint... 'by the way' instead of shouting, 'Look at me!')

♥ Garnish with cherry tomatoes and serve lightly chilled.

## Gemini – split baby imam bayildi

A heady mix of brashness and sensitivity, depth and frivolity, the Gemini has charm that is magnetic and charismatic.

**preparation 1¼ hours**

**2 small aubergines**
**sea salt**
**1 medium onion**
**2 garlic cloves**

♥ Preheat the oven to 200°C. Cut the aubergines in half lengthwise. Using a teaspoon, scoop out the flesh and discard.

♥ Sprinkle the hollowed-out hulls with salt and invert to allow any bitter juices to drain.

♥ Slice the onion into rings, as thin as you can manage. Slice the garlic as thinly. Peel, deseed and roughly chop the tomatoes.

**2 medium tomatoes**
**½ small wine glass of olive oil**
**½ bunch of parsley, finely chopped**
**1 large spoonful thick yoghurt**

♥ Sauté the onions in the oil over a moderate heat. They shouldn't colour, the aim is to persuade them to become floppy and soft.

♥ Stir in the garlic. Add the tomatoes with a sprinkle of salt and cook for about 3 minutes, stirring from time to time, until properly amalgamated. Stir in half the parsley and remove from the heat.

♥ Pile this into the aubergines and bake for about 15 minutes until tender. Remove from the oven and sprinkle with parsley.

-♥ Serve hot or cold, garnished with a spoonful of yoghurt.

# Cancer – asparagus purée with griddled sweet potato

Cancerian tenacity is legendary. A reflective temperament, coupled with an insightful mind and a fine understanding of perspective, allows Cancerians to take the rough with the smooth with alacrity.

**preparation 30 minutes**

**1 shallot**
**1 small glass of white wine or vinegar**
**sea salt and freshly ground black pepper**
**juice of ¼ lemon (if using wine)**
**100g unsalted (sweet) butter at room temperature**
**a bunch of green asparagus**
**1 orange-fleshed sweet potato or yam**

♥ Chop the shallot very finely and cook over moderate heat with the wine or vinegar and a good turn of the peppermill. Cook for about 3 minutes, until most of the wine has bubbled away. Add the lemon juice, if using wine.

♥ Add the butter little by little, whisking all the while. You should end up with a nicely amalgamated *beurre blanc*.

♥ Chop the asparagus into roughly 1cm lengths, the pieces getting smaller the further away from the head you go. Keep the woody stems to make stock, if you have time.

♥ Boil the asparagus in just enough water to cover, with a pinch of salt, until soft.

♥ Lift out the asparagus and place in a bowl. Process with a wand or in a food mill (see page 00), adding just enough of the cooking water to achieve a thick, smooth purée.

♥ Beat the asparagus purée into the *beurre blanc* and keep warm.

♥ Scrub the skin of the sweet potato, then slice it into thin discs.

♥ Heat a griddle pan until moderately hot and grill the discs (without oil) for about 2 minutes each side, until lined and crisp on the outside, soft and yielding in the middle. Season with salt and pepper.

♥ Reheat the asparagus *beurre blanc*. Place a spoon of it on each disc of grilled sweet potato or yam. Serve warm.

## Leo – emperor fish: fillets of gilt-head bream, lavender and fennel

Potential personified – no wonder that Leo people make natural leaders!

**preparation 20 minutes**

**sea salt and freshly ground black pepper**
**2 small fillets of gilt-head bream, skin on, and any residual bones removed (if unavailable, buy red mullet, but beware of small bones)**
**a little olive oil**
**1 small fennel bulb**
**1 small carrot**
**2 tablespoons lavender honey or good-quality clear (runny) honey**
**2 tablespoons white wine**
**a pinch of lavender flowers or a sprig of lavender, to garnish**

♥ Lightly salt the flesh of the fish.

♥ Slice the fennel very thinly lengthwise, discarding any woody core and dark green stems but reserving any feathery fronds for garnish. Cut the carrots into thin matchsticks.

♥ Heat the honey, wine and the carrots together gently for 3 minutes or so, stirring all the time. Season to taste and reserve.

♥ Heat a nonstick frying pan with a film of oil until medium-hot.

♥ Fry the fennel for about 5–6 minutes, turning once, until just softened, taking care not to burn it.

♥ Adding a little more oil if necessary, place the fish fillets in the same frying pan, skin side down, and cook for 2 minutes.

♥ Layer the still-warm fennel over a warm plate. Pour the honey/wine/carrot mixture into the middle. Place the fish fillets on top, one skin side up, the other down.

♥ Serve warm, garnished with fennel fronds, lavender and a good grind of pepper.

## Virgo – baby potatoes, truffled wild mushrooms

Conscientious and thorough, the twin qualities of ordered earthiness and (with their initial reserve put to one side!) abandoned sexuality make Virgoans dependable exciting lovers.

**preparation 25 minutes**

**200g baby potatoes, preferably Charlotte**
**sea salt and freshly ground black pepper**
**1 small onion**
**15g unsalted butter**
**75g wild mushrooms, or 65g field mushrooms plus 10g dried porcini (ceps), soaked for 10 minutes in 2**

♥ Scrub the skins of the potatoes, then boil them in salted water until cooked through.

♥ Meanwhile, chop the onion finely and sweat in the butter in a saucepan.

♥ Wipe the mushrooms with a damp tea towel, then slice neatly into 2mm slices.

♥ Add the wild mushrooms (or field mushrooms plus the soaked porcini) to the onion and stir well. Continue to cook on a low heat, giving the fungi a few turns of the peppermill.

♥ Place the hot potatoes in a bowl and crush them lightly with the back of a spoon.

tablespoons of hot water, then
drained, reserving the water)
a few shavings of fresh truffle or 1
teaspoon truffle paste or 10 drops
of white truffle oil
1 tablespoon chopped parsley

♥ At the last minute, mix the truffle/truffle paste/truffle oil into the mushroom mixture, then heap over the crushed potatoes and sprinkle with the parsley. Serve hot.

## Libra – chicken and tarragon frittata

Fair and firm and extremely companionable, Librans manage to balance careful husbandry of resources with unabashed hedonism!

**preparation 15 minutes**

4 medium eggs
100g cooked chicken, finely
shredded
2 sprigs of fresh tarragon, leaves
removed
sea salt and black pepper
50g unsalted butter

♥ Lightly beat the eggs.
♥ Mix in the chicken with half the tarragon and season lightly.
♥ Heat half the butter in a small nonstick omelette pan until the foam subsides.
♥ Spoon in half of the mixture and cook for about 1–2 minutes on each side, until golden brown.
♥ Serve immediately, garnished with half the remaining tarragon leaves.
♥ Wipe out the pan with kitchen roll and make the second frittata for yourself.

## Scorpio – prawn tails with spice-filled pipettes

Scorpios relish all that is straight and abhor sarcasm. Dynamic and forthright, they are possessed of legendary energy and a strong sense of the ridiculous.

**preparation 20 minutes**

4 large prawns, heads and shells on
2 tablespoons light soy sauce
1 tablespoon Worcestershire sauce
1 teaspoon red Tabasco sauce
1 teaspoon lemon juice

♥ If the prawns are raw, boil them for 6 minutes in salted water, then allow to cool and peel. If the prawns are bought ready-cooked, peel them, leaving the heads attached.
♥ Mix all the wet ingredients together thoroughly, then suck up into four 5ml pipettes.
♥ Make a deep incision, almost through to the other side, in the middle of each prawn tail.
♥ Place a sauce-filled pipette into this incision and serve, encouraging your guest to squeeze and remove the pipette before eating the succulent flesh.

## Sagittarius – braised red cabbage with fromage frais

Loyalty, stamina, incisiveness and sunny dispositions characterize Sagittarians. Their get-up-and-go is refreshing and invigorating!

**preparation 15 minutes**

1 small onion
50g unsalted butter
1 small red cabbage or ¼ large
1 small cooking apple
1 tablespoon brown sugar
2 tablespoons red wine vinegar
150ml hot vegetable stock
sea salt and freshly ground black pepper
10g finely grated fresh horseradish
100ml fromage frais

♥ Slice the onion, then fry in the butter in a deep casserole or pot over moderate heat, until pale golden brown.

♥ Cut the cabbage into thin ribbons, about 2mm wide, and add to the golden onion, then stir thoroughly.

♥ Peel the apple, then core and roughly chop. Add to the pot with the sugar and the vinegar. Stir until completely amalgamated, then add the hot vegetable stock. Season with salt to taste.

♥ Lower the heat and cook gently, tasting regularly, until the cabbage has just lost its raw, vegetal bite yet still retains some crunch.

♥ Beat the horseradish into the fromage frais and season with a few flecks of pepper.

♥ Place the still-warm red cabbage in a dish and fork through the flavoured fromage frais.

♥ Serve warm or lightly chilled.

## Capricorn – baked squash mashed with goats' cheese and pine nuts

Creative and richly varied, with the ability to remain unfazed by obstacles, the Capricorn climbs with alacrity to success.

**preparation about 1¼ hours**

1 small pumpkin or squash, such as red Kuri or green Hokkaido
40g unsalted butter
20g pine nuts
100g unrinded soft goats' cheese
sea salt
a few sprigs of parsley or chervil

♥ Preheat the oven to 200°C. Slice off the top of the pumpkin and reserve. With a spoon, scoop out all the pith and seeds and discard.

♥ Again with a spoon or a small knife, carefully remove the flesh from inside the squash, taking care not to puncture the skin.

♥ Chop the squash flesh small and cook it slowly in a saucepan with the butter until you can mash it.

♥ Meanwhile, in a hot dry frying pan, toast the pine nuts until golden - this takes only a few moments. Let them cool in a bowl.

♥ Combine the mashed pumpkin with the cheese by mashing with a fork. Taste and adjust the seasoning. Mix in the cooled pine nuts.

♥ Chop the herb, reserving one sprig, and add to the mix. Spoon the mix into the pumpkin and replace the lid.

♥ Bake for 10–15 minutes, until bubbling hot.

♥ Remove from the oven carefully and serve with the reserved herb.

# fresh artichokes with warm walnut and lemon vinaigrette

Artichokes make good food for lovers. They offer the perfect opportunity to share thoughts and mouthfuls.

### serves 2

**preparation about 1 hour**

**2 fresh artichokes, the stems peeled**

*for the vinaigrette*
**3 tablespoons walnuts**
**2 teaspoons salt**
**juice of 1 lemon**
**4 tablespoons good olive oil**

♥ Boil the artichokes whole in salted water acidulated with lemon juice, using a smaller lid to keep them submerged, for 45 minutes or until tender. Drain upside down.

♥ To make the vinaigrette, dry-fry the nuts over a moderate heat until tanned. When cool, crush to a thick chunky paste. Dissolve the salt in the lemon juice, then whisk into the oil. Add the walnuts and mix well. Warm the mixture in a small pan, taking great care not to let it boil.

♥ Serve in bowls or, better still, pour into the middle of the artichoke – you and your lover can then pull out the dressed leaves while undressing the artichoke. Later on, pull out the choke and remove any residual spikes. Now you've got to the heart of the matter.

---

# revueltos with wild greens and prawns

*Revueltos* are, if you like, Spanish scrambled eggs. All over Spain, bars and restaurants will make them to order for you in moments.

### serves 2

**preparation 20 minutes**

**1 cup of tiny cooked peeled prawns**
**1 tablespoon olive oil**
**½ small onion, finely chopped**
**salt and black pepper**
**4 large eggs at room temperature**
**2 tablespoons good olive oil**
**1 garlic clove, thinly sliced**

♥ Quickly sauté the prawns in the olive oil, with the chopped onion and salt, until warmed through.

♥ Crack the eggs into a bowl. Heat the good olive oil in a non-stick frying or omelette pan. When the oil shimmers and a haze starts to rise, throw in the prawns and garlic and stir, then pour in the eggs and stir vigorously with a wooden spoon. (In Spain, the cook uses a fast zig-zag movement, not letting the mixture rest even for a second.)

♥ Turn out the quivering *revueltos* on a plate, season with pepper and serve immediately. *Olé!*

# New Zealand green-lipped mussels with Gallipoli wine

This is written as a tribute to Gûven Nil, a man of great enthusiasm and compassion. Gûven loved to bring people together, which he did with charm, verve and panache. It is fitting, therefore, that his lasting memorial should be a great social and cultural catalyst, a wine he inspired and produced in Gallipoli, north-west Turkey.

The history of Gallipoli is bound up in the consciousness of New Zealand and Australia as well as Turkey. It also plays its part in the Greek myths. Gallipoli is where Xerxes crossed his army into Europe on a bridge of boats. Where Leander swam the Dardanelles to meet Hero in Sestos. Where Suleyman the Magnificent stood to command the view of countries and continents he was to conquer. And where, for nine months in 1915, a campaign was fought that claimed the lives of tens of thousands of brave young men, including the most promising Australians and the cream of Kiwis.

This finger of Turkey, now properly called Gelibolu, is defined by the Greek Aegean on one side and the Dardanelles on the other – one Christian, the other Muslim, yet it feels neither European nor Asian. At Kilid Bahir, the Narrows bring Europe to within 700 metres of Çanakkale in Asia, making it perhaps the most tantalizing stretch of water in the world: whoever commanded the Dardanelles held the key to Europe, Asia, Constantinople and the Black Sea. The geography of this spit makes Gelibolu an international land, with a cosmopolitan history.

Herodotus portrayed the Narrows as 'a wine-dark sea'. His allusion to the grape would have been easily understood by his contemporaries as the area produced some of the greatest wines of the known world – Odysseus toasted Athena with splendid Callipolis wine at nearby Philadelphia, having been victorious over the Thracians - the peninsula had been cultivating grapes of quality since 3000 BC. Callipolis wine was drunk in Troy and Marathon, and later wherever the civilized cadres of the Ottoman Empire were posted.

By the end of the 19th century, however, wine-making in Gelibolu was in decline. The last Ottoman emperors cultivated European tastes, following French and Italian fashions, and thus wines from those lands, no matter how poorly they travelled, were considered superior to those that were home-grown. There is a nice irony in an ancient society toasting its sunset years with what would have been then thought of as New World wines...

Early in the First World War, Winston Churchill asserted that taking charge of the Dardanelles would cause Istanbul to 'fall like a house of cards', resulting in the removal of Turkey (an ally of the Germans) from the war, and affording the

Russians a vital ice-free sea supply route. The battle for Gallipoli was essentially mismanaged by the British Allies, and made the reputation of Mustafa Kemal Ataturk, whose charisma and drive were to inspire the modern Turkish state. Commonwealth states, in particular Australia, New Zealand and Canada, were proud to volunteer their most able young men, acts which signalled their coming of nationhood, and presaged the dissolution of the British Empire.

With the straits heavily mined, and the Allied commanders hamstrung by political pressures and poor communication, a decision was made to land the Commonwealth troops from the Aegean side of the peninsula (for which woefully inaccurate maps were held), thence to fight their way across to the Dardanelles. These boys were as unprepared for amphibious landing as their commanders-in-chief were inept: landing on tiny beaches, they made easy meat for the Turkish artillery, perched patiently on high, able to see every troop movement approaching their shores.

Those that made it past Hell Spit or the carnage of Anzac Cove and up the cliffs at Çanak Bair were destined to live the next months in a surreal world of danger and dysentery, in a city of trenches with names such as Piccadilly Circus and Plymouth Avenue. Often only spitting distance away from enemy lines, soldiers on both sides were ordered to fight futile skirmishes that could yield only a few feet of earth, often to be relinquished in the next battle. Yet there existed a spirit of mutual respect between the opposing soldiers. In addition, as General Sir Ian Hamilton, the benighted Allied commander, noted, there was often to be found an atmosphere akin to joy on the peninsula. Here men were relieved of the everyday cares of their previous existence and could revel in an unparalleled *esprit de corps*:

'There are poets and writers who see naught in war but carrion, filth, savagery and horror... They refuse war the credit of being the only exercise in devotion on the large scale existing in this world. The superb moral victory over death leaves them cold. Each one to his taste. To me this [the bridgehead at Hellespont] is no valley of death – it is a valley brim full of life at its highest power. Men live through more in five minutes on that crest than they do in five years at home. Ask the brothers of these very fighters – Calgoorlie or Coolgardie miners – to do one quarter of the work and to run one hundredth of the risk on a wages basis – instantly there would be a riot. But not here – not a murmur, not a question, only a radiant force of camaraderie in action.'

The international Lausanne Agreement of 1919 ensured that the Gelibolu peninsula would become and remain a national park, dedicated to the memory of the young men whose remains rested there. With infinite care, the Commonwealth Graves Commission maintains numerous beautiful cemeteries, each sensitively designed by Sir John Burnet. The French have their own glorious memorial and the Turks have built a stunning arched structure to commemorate their fallen. The atmosphere on the peninsula, however, is not morbid. The songbirds sing (oh, how they sing!) and the ground is fertile, yielding grapes, olives, cotton and delicious sweet almonds. A cemetery surrounded by fields of yellow sunflowers, their heads turning towards the heavens, makes it easy to believe that its inhabitants did not die in vain. A memorial at Anzac Cove glorifies the deeds of a brave generation and bears Ataturk's words of respect and reconciliation:

'Those heroes that shed their blood and lost their lives... you are now lying in the soil of a friendly country, therefore rest in peace. There is no difference between the Johnnies and the Mehmets to us where they lie side by side here in this country of ours... To the mothers who sent their sons from faraway countries, wipe away your tears: your sons are now lying in our bosom and are at peace. After having lost their lives on this land they have become our sons as well.'

The intention enshrined in the Lausanne Agreement was to forbid desecration of the historic land. This, in turn, militated against inward investment. The result is a region that, while retaining its due dignity, has also suffered acute population decline, not to mention the loss of local crafts, in particular the wine-making so spurned by the last sultans.

On to the set of Gelibolu's recent history step two men: Gûven Nil and

Ahmet Kutman. In 1926, Ahmet's father, Nihat Bey, was requested by Ataturk himself to recommence viniculture around the Dardanelles. Ataturk's plan was that Nihat Kutman's work should create positive links between the thrusting new state and its vinous traditions, and was a calculated move away from a Muslim orthodoxy that frowned on wine's associations with intoxication. Nihat Bey rejuvenated ancient vineyards in the area around Mûrefte, whose fruits had been extolled in a previous age by Darius the Mede (passing on his way to fight the Athenians). He set up the Doluca company, whose name today is synonymous with Turkish wine.

Ahmet Kutman, a graduate of Istanbul's Robert College, returned to Turkey in 1967, having studied oenology and viticulture at the University of California, and set about the modernization and marketing of Doluca wines. The company now produces 10 million bottles of wine every year. Ahmet's room-mate at Robert College was Gûven Nil. A basketball-loving, go-getting dynamo, He was to become Turkey's pre-eminent private banker. Gûven was that rare combination, hard businessman and soft romantic.

His business success fuelled an interest in wines that was informed by a series of visits to France and the Napa Valley, an appreciation of top quality and a love of good living. His lasting legacy, he decided, was to be in the founding of a wine of international renown, a project that would be difficult, expensive and time-consuming: in essence, his perfect challenge. In the late 1980s, Gûven approached his old room-mate with a plan of his dream, which chimed with Ahmet's desire to venture out of the mass market, and the Sarafin label was born. Gûven would establish the vineyards and Ahmet would assume responsibility for the wine-making.

Gûven Nil was deeply attracted to the atmosphere of the Dardanelles: it was a place where great men had performed great deeds. His business mind was drawn to possibilities of finding affordable land and a willing workforce, while his emotions sought to re-energize and redeem the land where once great wines had been made and, later, where men had been sacrificed. Ever the enthusiast, he bought up parcels of land and planted nearly 80 hectares of Old and New World rootstock, as well as 7,000 Ayvalik olive trees and 10,000 sweet almond trees. The Kutmans' factory at Mûrefte was extended and updated to include a boutique winery for Sarafin; in place of pride, a cellar of French Limousin oak barrels.

Gûven planted Cabernet and Merlot, Shiraz and Cabernet Franc, and Chardonnay and Sauvignon Blanc grapes. What he, or Ahmet, could not have expected was the fact that their wines, produced in areas where the Gallipoli Campaign had been most hard-fought, have not only redeemed the land, but also assumed a character that is uncannily Antipodean. Those familiar with, say, the wines produced by Michael Seresin in Marlborough, New Zealand, will recognize the same nose-note of mimosa and long melon finish as in Sarafin's Sauvignon Blanc. (Seresin has recently planted Tuscan olive trees on his land, the oil of which has the same depth of flavour and round olive fruit as that pressed from Gûven's Ayvalik trees.)

The parallels do not stop there. It took a certain peacetime bravery for Gûven Nil and Ahmet Kutman to commit $10 million, as well as their time and energy, to a project with an unknown future, especially in an economic climate that rewards short-term investment but often penalizes long-sighted projects. And unlimited reserves of bravery were common among the wartime volunteers willing to leave home and step into the unknown in the name of pride and for the sake of their nations.

The Gelibolu peninsula has honourable mentions in the myths of ancient Greece and modern Turkey: to Australians and New Zealanders, the name Gallipoli is synonymous with national identity. What better way to toast a heroic past and a Brave New World than with a glass of Sarafin and the Turkish toast 'Sherefe!', 'To honour!'

This recipe seeks to fuse the characters and flavours from two seemingly disparate parts of the world that share a proud history. It is dedicated to Gûven Nil, whose actions have spanned East and West, and both hemispheres. Gûven died, aged 56, in 2001, while playing his weekly game of basketball. He would have loved this dish!

## serves 4

**preparation about 25 minutes**

4 garlic cloves, very thinly sliced
a knob of butter
1 teaspoon sugar
1 teaspoon lemon juice
2 hot peppers (1 green and 1 red)
1 small onion, very finely chopped
2 glasses of Sarafin Sauvignon Blanc (one for the pot, one for you)
1.5 kg New Zealand green-lipped mussels, rinsed clean
fresh country bread, to serve

♥ Gently sauté the garlic in a little butter. As the garlic becomes faintly coloured, add the sugar dissolved in the lemon juice. Continue to cook until the liquid has all but disappeared.

♥ Slice the peppers lengthwise and, in order to hint rather than scream about heat, remove all the seeds and the pith. Remember to wash your hands after this, and do not touch your eyes or your flies. Slice the peppers into the thinnest ribbons possible.

♥ Rub a thin film of butter around the base and sides of a saucepan which has a lid. Throw the onion and peppers into the pan with the wine and simmer gently for about 2 minutes, until the onion has started to soften. Add the garlic and the mussels and cover. Turn the heat up to high and steam the mussels for 3–4 minutes, shaking the pan from time to time.

♥ Serve in bowls with some cooking liquid and hunks of bread.

# tagliata with peppery rocket leaves

Tuscans have bred Chianina cows in the hills behind Florence for centuries. *Bistecca alla Fiorentina* is their way of cooking T-bone – over charcoal and anointed with olive oil. Cutting rump steak into ribbons (*tagliata*) is one of the delicious things that Tuscans like to do with their beef.

serves 2

**preparation about 15 minutes**

2 rump steaks, each about 175g
  a little olive oil
sea salt and freshly ground black
  pepper
1 tablespoon red wine vinegar
2 tablespoons good olive oil
100g rocket leaves

♥ Trim the steaks of absolutely all fat and massage the meat with a little olive oil, salt and pepper.

♥ Heat a dry griddle pan until it smokes. Put the steaks on it and reduce the heat to medium. Sprinkle with salt. Cook for about 2 minutes, then carefully turn and season again.

♥ While the steaks are cooking, make a dressing by mixing 1 teaspoon of salt into the vinegar and then whisking the good olive oil into that. Season with pepper and toss the rocket leaves in it to coat well.

♥ When the steaks are done (the inside should still be very pink, the outside nicely grilled), cut them into short, thick ribbons.

♥ Serve the *tagliata* over the dressed rocket salad.

# milk of almonds with attar of roses

As a flower's fragrance precedes it, so an essential oil captures its soul. Essential oils were probably discovered by chance in 10th-century Persia by Ibn Sena (Avicenna), the greatest Eastern philosopher physician. Roses were considered essential in the attempt to transmute base metals into gold, and Ibn Sena's alchemical experiments required roses to be placed in retorts and heated. The resultant distilled liquids were thus imbued with the flower's fragrance, crowned by a filmy cap of essential oil, the soul of the rose. By the end of that century, flower waters and essential oils were known throughout the Arab-speaking world.

The Mughal Indians discovered rose oil at the wedding of Shah Jehan to Noor, for whose love he was later to build the Taj Mahal. Emperor Jehan commanded that the moat surrounding his castle be filled with rose petals, over which wedding guests were ferried. As the sun beat down, it caused a natural distillation of the flowers, the oil was skimmed from the surface and offered as a bridal gift, and the rose water used to sanctify the bridal ceremony.

Rose oil is still given as a wedding present in Bulgaria, home (many would say) to the world's best roses for rose oil. Bulgarian otto (or attar) of roses is so thick that it solidifies at anything below room temperature, and it fetches a fabulous price – up to £300 an ounce! In the last hundred years, Bulgarian families have settled the fertile valleys around Burdur in south-west Anatolia and started to grow roses on terraced hillsides.

I learned the following dish in the home of Hüseyin Tezcan in Basmakçi village, about 2 hours' drive from Burdur at the end of a ribbon of a road that threads its way through the impressive countryside. Basmakçi is too far from town, and its fields too inaccessible, to make carting chemicals there profitable, so the elders have agreed to farm completely organically. The village has two mosques but no shop, unless you count the confectionery kiosk adjoining the tea house, and about 40 wood-built houses nestling into the hillside. The air is crisp and cleansing, the light pure and hard.

I visited in autumn – everywhere people were drying strings of peppers, beans and okra for the winter. Hüseyin's daughters, Radiye (The Blessed One) and Burcu (The One Who Smells Nice), served us delicious sweet sage tea. His wife Sukran (Gratitude) produced a beautiful, simple evening meal: tarama, a delicious pounded wheat soup, served with cızlama, wholemeal bread made in a round tin and served to table sizzling ('cızlama') with butter. Fresh green beans came with short-grain rice and a wonderful zingy salad of juicy tomatoes with sweet onion and green chilli.

The feast was laid out on a low-table (sofra), at which we knelt, the food so fresh and delicious as to render me oblivious to aching hips and knees. All the food was served with wafer-thin saç bread in a living room adorned with wall-hung plastic tablecloths, Sukran's embroidery and lit by a single light bulb. Yellow watermelon followed, from Hüseyin's field, then this dessert of milk of almonds, topped with a single drop of powerful rose otto.

The Tezcans are proud that their rose oil, made in the fields with a mobile pot-bellied still, has been deemed good enough for Dr Hauschka, the legendary brand of creams and lotions that lustre the bodies of the world's top models. This dish might even do for your insides what Dr Hauschka's does for their skin!

For those of you who, like me, are touched by such things, you might like to know that I stayed overnight with the Tezcans and woke early the next morning to the sound of Huseyin knocking walnuts off the tree overhanging his courtyard, which he served for breakfast, together with thick, aromatic honey, strained yoghurt, warm spelt bread, just-laid eggs, goats' cheese, sweet juicy tomatoes and lemon balm tea. That's what I call a Good Morning!

makes 10 small sweet,
rich portions (perfect
with a cup of strong
coffee or herbal tea,
or as a dessert)

**preparation 15 minutes,
plus 1 hour's chilling and
cooling**

250g blanched almonds
250g caster sugar
a few drops of attar of roses

♥ Place the almonds and 850ml water in a food processor, and whiz together to an almond milk. Let stand in a bowl in the fridge for 1 hour.
♥ Strain the milk through muslin or a very fine sieve, and add the sugar. Simmer the mixture for 30 minutes in a wide pan, stirring occasionally, until it thickens enough to coat the back of a spoon.
♥ Decant into a serving bowl, or individual glasses, and let cool.
♥ Serve with a drop of attar adorning each serving.

*If you'd like to experience a taste of village life in Anatolia, or are interested in discovering how some of Turkey's inner secrets may be the same as yours, then try sending an email to munirakd@e-kolay.net, or telephone 00 90 212 230 0213 and ask for Münir Akdogan (whose name translates as 'Enlightened White Eagle').*

# grapefruit with Campari and crystallized ginger

First, pour yourself a nice long Campari soda. Then sit down for a while and contemplate this recipe:

♥ One or more grapefruit, peeled and cut into segments, or simply sliced in half, depending on how long ago (and how long!) you made that drink.
♥ The segments should be soaked in Campari for at least an hour, and maybe overnight; the halves should sit in a saucer of the drink for the same period.
♥ Serve chilled, with finely chopped crystallized ginger and perhaps a little unrefined sugar.

# faloodeh sib

Inspired by Iran, this dish serves 4 as a light dessert, or as a
palate refresher between courses.

**preparation 20 minutes**

2 large dessert apples
juice of 2 lemons, strained
3 tablespoons rose water
2 cups of crushed ice
about 4 tablespoons caster sugar

♥ Peel and core the apples, then coarsely grate them directly into
the lemon juice, to prevent browning.

♥ Add the rose water and gently stir in the crushed ice.

♥ Add caster sugar to taste, and serve immediately.

# chapter six
## eating your way to health

In meditation, the idea is to empty the mind of the daily chitter-chatter in order to allow fresh thoughts to flourish. An analogy is with a glass of pure fresh water: no matter how crystal-clear, how perfectly chilled, or how sweet the water is, the glass must be drained in order to not become stale and dusty, and for its contents to have their desired effect, and to invite fresh water to be poured. So it is with food.

Someone once told me that food should not be taken until the previous meal has been fully digested, which makes sense, but (let's face it) has little practical application for food lovers like us. I don't know about you, but I am perfectly able to spend unlimited time justifying food desire. My mind, so expensively trained in rhetoric and sophistry, asks why would God have made food so delicious if we are not to love it and honour it and ... eat it? Mind you, the same mind is also fickle and callow, and while encouraging and fomenting food fantasies, is happy to introduce the concept of guilt, which overrides said fantasies, and as such keeps itself over-employed as head honcho.

Therefore, if positive health is to be attained and maintained, a balance must be found between the mental tensions of desire and guilt. My gut feeling is that it's perfectly necessary to indulge in fine food, but not all the time (as it stops being a treat), or too much (as it burdens the system), or while worrying about it (unless masochism is your thing). Wearing a Versace hair shirt is acceptable on occasion, but it should not be eaten.

The fact is that inner peace comes only when the digestion is healthy. The body is a factory that has a certain amount of energy available to it for performing its functions, the majority of which concern processing food. The factory's workforce cannot be expected always to work overtime: it reacts by either sacrificing quality, demanding higher pay or going on strike. If the body is not to become reliant on quick-fix remedies, the solution is to allow it certain periods of calmness, during which essential maintenance can take place, and the digestive system is afforded a holiday.

Different folk have different theories as to the best way to rest the system. At places like the Meyer clinic in Austria, your £500 a week buys a range of healthy spa treatments, and the chance to retrain the digestion by eating pretty much only thin soup, yoghurt and stale bread, each chunk of which must be masticated 50 times. Stern nurses with scraped-back hair, white coats and sensible shoes are on hand to make sure that guests don't stray into butter-biscuit territory, or take too much pleasure in their punishment.

Then there is the proliferation of 'diets', which, in the modern world, are followed instead of common sense, and sometimes in place of religion. If we're told often enough that we're weak, then sooner or later we'll start to believe it! This doctor or that clinic has only to tell us never to eat wheat, or to eat only wheat, for their books to become bestsellers and for adherents to proselytize about them with fundamentalist fervour. This comes as no surprise, as calorie-counting and food fads work by reinforcing reliance on themselves, some systems forcing novices to attend weekly communal ritual humiliations, others training the mind to perform that function for them. The problem derives in part from over-concentration to the point of infatuation, of the theory being mistaken for the substance, and is driven by a certain unwholesome self-centredness.

I hope that you'll enjoy this illustration from Rumi's *Mathnawi, Book 6*, here rendered in a version by Coleman Barks:

## Dalqak's Message

The King of Tirmid
Had urgent business in Samarqand.

He needed a courier to go there and
return in five days. He offered many
rewards to anyone who would make
the journey -   horses, servants, gold
and the robes of honour.
                    Dalqak, the court
clown, was out in the country when
he heard of this.
He quickly mounted a horse and rode
towards town.
He rode furiously. Two horses
dropped dead of exhaustion under his
whip.
                    He arrived
covered with dust at some ungodly
hour, demanding an audience with the
King.

A panic swept the city. What calamity
could be so imminent that Dalqak,
the buffoon,should be so distraught?
Everyone gathered at the palace.
          'An evil omen is upon us!'
'Something has certainly been spilled
on the rug this time!'

          The King himself was worried.
'What is it, Dalqak?'
                    Whenever anyone
asked Dalqak for particulars about

anything, he first put his finger to
his lips,
          Shhhhhhhh....
                    Everyone got very quiet.
Dalqak made another gesture as
though to say he needed more time
to catch his breath.

Another long wait. No one had ever
seen Dalqak like this. Usually he was
a constant stream of new jokes.
Usually, the King would be laughing
so hard he'd fall on the floor holding
his stomach. This quietness was
very odd and foreboding.
                    Everyone's
worst fears came up.
          'The tyrant from Khwarism
is coming to kill us!'
                    'Dalqak, tell what it is!'

'I was far from court when I heard
that you needed a courier, someone
who could go to Samarqand and
come back in five days.'
                              'Yes!
"I hurried here to tell you
that I will not be able to do it.'
                              'What!'
'I don't have the stamina or the
agility.
Don't expect me to be the one.'

You'll have to ask yourself whether Dalqak is the food, the dieter,
willpower - or the diet - I'm off for a snack!

# Grandma's chicken soup with almond dumplings

My mother is Marlene Gould, and her story is beautiful. Her father, Yacoub Yousefi, was born in an Iranian town called Kashan. Kashan is bordered on one side by the Zagros Mountains, the other by deserted salt marshes. Life in Kashan was tough: the town was known for its cotton traders, its silk carpets, its roses – and its scorpions. In 1912, when he was 15 years old, Yacoub's job was to stencil on to bales of cotton the word 'Manchester', at that time the cotton metropolis of the world. Manchester, he reasoned, having to stencil so many bales, must be a very rich country. He would go there and make his fortune.

Cue gales of laughter from friends of family. No one left Kashan, unless on a trading trip to nearby Qom. For that matter, few visited, unless on specific business – so going to 'Manchester'?! Young Yacoub was undeterred, and with the tiny amount of money that his mother, Sara, had saved for his eventual wedding day, he set out walking to find his fortune.

His journey lasted two years, and in 1914 Yacoub Yousefi presented himself
at the southern English port of Southampton. Repeating his Manchester
mantra, he was given a train ticket to his destination and a new name:
Jeff Joseph.

Jeff loved Manchester. In contrast to Kashan, it was cold and wet, and
big and bustling, and provided endless possibilities for an enterprising young
man. He arrived just as war was declared, and built a textile business, starting
with a barrow selling balls of string fashioned from stripped-down cotton waste,
and graduating through handkerchiefs to owning his own warehouse.

Jeff Joseph prospered greatly, and imported his brothers and several
cousins to share his comfortable new life. He married the daughter of
Manchester's most eminent shipper of Egyptian cotton, thus acquiring
extended family in Egypt, Syria, Lebanon and Turkey. Having had none of his
own, Jeff Joseph's commitment to education was quite passionate, and he
assumed responsibility for the schooling of not only his own five children but
of countless others. His legacy lives on at the Jeff Joseph High School in
south Manchester.

My mother was his middle daughter, and in 1957 she married my father,
David. Dad's grandfather, a young man with a flaming red beard, was from
somewhere within the Russian Pale of Settlement, most probably in what is now
Ukraine. Fleeing pogroms, he had bought a steerage-class ticket to New York,
boarding the boat in Danzig (Gdansk). On reaching Liverpool, England, the
unscrupulous captain bellowed 'New York!' and off filed his obedient
passengers. The boat was on its way back to Danzig before anybody had
cottoned on.

Given the new name of David Davies, my great-grandfather, with
magnificent irony, made a living as a Cossack rider in the circus. His family
proliferated, and my grandmother Esther was taught to remain conscious of
her Eastern European roots by preparing foods from the *shtetl* (village) that
had been home to her forebears.

Friday night dinner was the grandest meal of the week. The family
budget allowed for a chicken each Friday, not one bit of which would be
wasted: it would be transformed into a golden soup, the meat to be served
for a main course, the bones and trimmings to become stock. It was inevitable
that when my father married Marlene, no matter her exotic eastern ways with
rice and kebabs, with pitta breads and roasted pumpkin seeds, that she
would learn how to make chicken soup. Here it is, the soup that sustains,
Marlene's penicillin!

serves 6

**preparation about 3¼ hours plus overnight cooling**

**1 small chicken**
**4 large carrots**
**6 celery stalks**
**1 large onion**
**a pinch of saffron**
**sea salt and freshly ground black pepper**
**1 nest of vermicelli**

*for the kneidlach (dumplings)*
**150g fine matzo meal**
**2 tablespoons ground almonds**
**1 tablespoon light vegetable oil**
**2 eggs**

♥ Make the soup the day before: rinse the bird inside and out. Cut the carrots and celery into thick chunks. Cut the onion in half.

♥ Put the bird and the vegetables in a large pan which has a tight-fitting lid and just cover with cold water. Bring to the boil.

♥ As the water boils, remove 2 tablespoons of it, place in a bowl and steep the saffron in it for 10 minutes.

♥ After about 15 minutes of steady boiling, skim the scum from the top of the water, then season with salt and pepper. Cover the bird, lower the heat to a slow simmer and cook for 2½ hours. Allow the chicken to cool in the soup.

♥ Remove and reserve the bird, and strain the liquid through a colander. You might like to slice the meat thinly and return it to the liquid, then serve it as a separate main course, or keep it for another dish.

♥ Slice the cooked carrots into thin pennies and add them to the liquid.

♥ Place the chicken soup in the refrigerator overnight – the next morning a thick layer of fat will have formed on top, remove it with a spoon. (It can be good to spoon the fat (*schmalz* in Yiddish) on dishes of fried food, but only if you think your arteries can stand it.)

♥ To make the *kneidlach*, have ready a pan of hot water. Mix the matzo meal with the ground almonds, season with salt and moisten the mix with vegetable oil. Beat both the eggs and incorporate them into the mixture. Work just enough hot water into the mixture to make it hold together. With wet hands, roll the dough into balls the size of small walnuts.

♥ Poach the *kneidlach* in boiling salted water for about 10 minutes. Remove with a slotted spoon, ready to be reheated in the soup.

♥ Heat the soup to simmering point, add the vermicelli and cook until soft. Add the sliced chicken (if using) and the *kneidlach*, and heat through.

♥ Serve hot, with a grandmother's blessing.

# pam b'oli

This delicious real food is eaten all over the Mediterranean. I first enjoyed its sunny flavour on the island of Majorca as a child.

serves 1

**preparation about 10 minutes**

1 thick slice of coarse crusty white bread
1 garlic clove, cut in half
a slash of olive oil
½ very fresh tomato
a small sprinkle of sea salt

♥ Grill the bread on both sides until golden as suntanned skin.

♥ Rub one side firmly with garlic. Splash on a few zigzags of olive oil.

♥ Rub the coarse, slick fragrant surface with the soft, sensual tomato, then sprinkle with salt.

♥ Devour, remembering the tone poem on the sound of 'A' by Lorca, in a conscious reflection of the Arab Andalusian poet kings of the 9th and 10th centuries...

'La Muchacha Dorada/ Se Bañaba/ En el Agua/ Y el Agua/ Se doraba', Federico García Lorca, *El Diván de Tamarit*

# bitter leaf salad with superfood dressing

We tend not to eat enough bitter foods: a shame, as they stimulate bile and, in turn, digestion. This virtuous dish combines the benefits of three bitter leaves, and dressing made from green 'superfoods' (nutrient-rich) and perfectly balanced oil, sharpened with lemon juice and sweetened with mint leaves.

### serves 4

**preparation 10 minutes**

2 tablespoons hemp seeds
sea salt
1 head of white Belgian chicory
1 head of curly endive
1 head of radicchio di Treviso
1 tablespoon chopped fresh mint

💙 Dry-fry the hemp seeds until they start to pop, and then season with salt.

💙 Arrange the salad leaves on the serving plate(s).

💙 Make the dressing: blend the superfood powder in the oil, then whisk in the lemon juice.

💙 Strew the dressed salad with mint leaves and hemp seeds, if using them.

*for the superfood dressing*
**1 scant tablespoon
chlorella/spirulina powder
4 tablespoons cold-pressed hemp
oil or Udo's Choice oil
4 tablespoons lemon juice**

Both of the green superfoods, chlorella and spirulina, are available from good health stores. Being algae, they have a pronounced seaweed flavour; if you prefer otherwise, choose wheatgrass or barley greens powder instead. Cold-pressed hemp oil and Udo's Choice oil have very attractive nutritional profiles, the latter having been developed by a man who revels in the name of Dr Udo Erasmus, author of the jolly *Fats That Heal, Fats That Kill.*

# d'ukkah

The food of the poor in Cairo, freshly mixed by street vendors, *d'ukkah* is served in paper cones, to be mixed with a little oil before hot bread is dipped into it. While a delicious way to eat this dish, *d'ukkah* is equally useful stirred into salad dressings. My grandmother's family were Alexandrian cotton traders. This, therefore, is the Anzarut version of *d'ukkah*, which makes quite a large quantity, but keeps well in an airtight jar.

**350g sesame seeds
250g coriander seeds
120g shelled hazelnuts
120g ground cumin
120g za'atar (wild thyme – dried
thyme or oregano serve nearly as
well)
2 teaspoons coarse salt
1 teaspoon coarsely ground black
pepper**

♥ Dry-fry all the ingredients separately until they smell good to you.
♥ Put them all together in a big bowl and pound them until they become a coarse powder. (Food processors are not recommended here, as they tend to turn the mixture into an oily mass.) If in doubt, roll all the ingredients in a large tea towel and beat them with a rolling pin.

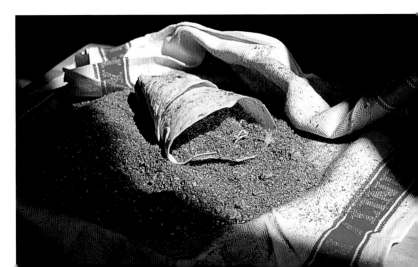

# nutty quinoa pilaf

Quinoa (pronounced keen-wa by the food fashionistas) is billed as the 'mystical grain of the Andes'. Well, whether it was eaten by Incas or not, what's for sure is that it is a handy grain to have in the larder. It's useful nutritionally, as (along with millet alone) quinoa is an alkali-forming grain, and is thus extremely digestible. It also has an excellent protein profile – in other words, it helps you to stay up, and is easy to keep down. As a good food, quinoa has other uses too. Its translucent crescent-figured grains have a less pronounced flavour than, say, wheat or rice, and therein lies its strength. Quinoa's gentle, desultory character serves to amplify the flavours that it accompanies, like a mirror that flatters a waistline and makes a face glow with health.

I am reminded of a poem, not wholly appropriate, but nonetheless beautifully drawn, and obviously written by a man whose somewhat tart tone to his lover bespeaks a beleaguered digestion that would doubtless have benefited from the occasional plate of quinoa:

'I send to you this marvellous mirror...
then you will have to admit
how beautiful you are
and will forgive me
the passion I feel for you.

And though your image is elusive,
it is still more accessible,
more benevolent,
and a better keeper of promises
than you are!'

Ibn al-Sabuni (Seville, 13th century), Poems of Arab Andalucia

serves 4

**preparation about 40 minutes**

**4 cups of quinoa**
**8 cups of boiling lightly salted water or stock**
**1 cup of hazelnuts, toasted and splintered**
**a smear of vegetable oil**

♥ Add the quinoa to the boiling liquid in the pan. Cover, turn the heat to low and cook for 15 minutes.

♥ Most of the liquid should have been absorbed and the quinoa should have swelled to show off its crescent markings. If still sloppy, raise the heat and cook uncovered for a few minutes more.

♥ Add most of the hazelnuts and fork through, then leave the grain to rest, covered, for 5 minutes.

♥ Pack into small lightly oiled bowls. Serve unmoulded, scattered with the remaining hazelnuts, as an accompaniment to quietly flavoured dishes, such as the Healing Sole opposite.

# healing herb and ginger-stuffed sole

As the multinational conglomerates start to push Functional Foods into consumers' awareness, the opportunity arises also to inform our home cooking with the virtues of healing herbs. Echinacea well deserves its reputation as a promoter of T-cell regeneration, but doesn't come top of anybody's taste list. This recipe seeks to civilize its uncouth flavour by marrying it with ginger.

For the scientists among us, I realize that this cooking method renders the herb's activity less potent, but if we were to see everything in purely scientific terms, then life would have to be led rather differently. You might argue that science is predicated on the ability to analyse, and therefore that which is empirically provable is concrete, irrevocable. But even though science is the child of wonder, scientific thought has become widely diverted, with experiments being too often conducted with a result in mind: to prove a point (and flatter an ego). It is essential, though, to discriminate between (and celebrate the marriage of) mind and soul. If you like, then, science only knows what it thinks, but by adding heart into the formula, you may get to know what you feel. What I believe is that your decision to use echinacea in this recipe adds to the energetic quality of the dish – just try it and see how it makes you feel...

serves 4

**preparation 1 hour**

8 small skinless fillets of sole

*for the poaching stock*
4 tablespoons Echinacea purpurea
4 cups of just-boiled water
1 cup of organic white wine
sea salt and freshly ground black pepper

*for the stuffing*
2 cm root ginger
a little boiling water
2 celery stalks, cut into small dice
(plus the chopped leaves for garnish)

♥ First make the poaching stock, steep the echinacea in the just-boiled water, covered, for 40 minutes or longer. Drain, mix with the wine and season.

♥ Prepare the stuffing, peel the ginger and cut it into tiny dice, then soak it for 5 minutes in just enough boiling water to cover. Drain, mix with the diced celery and season.

♥ Split each sole fillet down the middle. Place a little of the stuffing on each piece of sole and roll it up, securing the paupiette with a cocktail stick.

♥ Place the paupiettes in a pan and pour over the poaching liquid. Bring to the boil, cover the pan and remove from the heat. Leave for 5 minutes.

♥ Remove the paupiettes from the stock and serve, sprinkled with celery leaves and liberally splashed with reheated poaching stock.

# green tea sorbet with mint leaves

Tea has been taken in China for three millennia, and it's from the *Camellia sinensis* bush that all the world's teas stem. Lao-tzu, the father of Taoism, was calling tea the 'elixir of immortality' in the first century BC, when green tea would have been frothed in a bowl using a short bamboo whisk, just as the Aztecs were whisking their chocolate and offering it to their gods. Give or take 900 years later, the Taoist poet Lu-yu wrote his Cha-jing treatise, which remains the wellspring of tea technique and philosophy. Lu-yu is now known as Cha-zu, the tea genie, and his image adorns Hong Kong teahouses to this day. To Cha-zu, a cup of tea was the mirror of his soul; to his followers, the ritual making and taking of tea symbolized poetry and beauty, strength and determination.

A century later, tea drinking was introduced to Japan by the Buddhist monk Eichu (Bless you). He introduced tea to the monasteries, where its reviving effects made light the work of studying even the heaviest of texts. Eichu infused the tea ceremony with four values: *kin*, *kei*, *sei* and *joku* – reverence, respect, purity and tranquillity. The Emperor became a devotee, and the tea ritual came to resemble a distillation of the social mores of the time, with its carefully prescribed warmed tea pots, matching porcelain tea sets, and so on.

Green and black teas are from the same leaf, but are subjected to different post-harvest treatments. All tea is picked as very young leaves and flowers. Correction – tea is never picked, always plucked. In fact, Ming Dynasty emperors decreed that their green tea might only be plucked by virgins with sweet breath, to whom would be supplied a fresh dress and new gloves every day. The Chinese passed on the wisdom to Japan that the purity and freshness of tea were second only to the quality of water with which it was made. Great care was taken to ensure that tea water was drawn from impeccable sources – melted snow, fast-flowing rivers, or fresh sweet-water springs being always preferred over well water.

This recipe calls for green tea. Fashionable again of late, and media-hyped with properties ranging from detoxifying to cancer-curing, green tea (when properly prepared) remains a life-affirming brew. The ritualized hospitality of tea-making in Japan revolves around sharing and creating hospitality inside and outside of the self. The tea-maker's role, and that of the guest, is to pay attention to the tea-making procedure, and to be conscious of the space in which the tea is drunk. Traditionally, the role of the *Chashitsu* (teahouse) has been to provide a refuge from the stresses of city life. The mark of a good teahouse is a beautiful ordered environment, from which one leaves calmer, re-energized by the visit.

Elements of the contemplative calm of the *Chashitsu* should be present when you take tea. Water quality is essential in good tea-making: water must be freshly drawn before each making. The very best green teas are imported from China, Taiwan, Korea, Vietnam and Japan. Should you be able to find a traditionally grown tea from any of these countries, it should deliver you sweet herbal accents and a depth of flavour absent in commercial brands.

In making green tea well, the secret lies in water temperature. Generally, the better the tea, the cooler the water. For instance, the Dong Yang Estate produces some of Korea's finest *nokcha* (green tea). Wild flowers flourish between the rows of *nochka* bushes – a sure sign that the tea is produced without chemical intervention. When infused with water at a mere 70°C, Dong Yang tea makes a drink full of natural caramel sweetness, with an earthy biscuit fragrance.

Green tea of this quality should be drunk sitting down. Thus the time you invest in making it and taking it is repaid in refreshed composure. Before you make this recipe, or while the tea is infusing, why not treat yourself to a reflective cup of Lao-tzu's elixir of immortality?

### serves 4

**preparation about 3¼ hours, plus several hours' freezing**

**3 tablespoons white granulated sugar**
**3 heaped tablespoons good green tea**
**juice of 1 lemon**
**8 beautiful fresh mint leaves**

♥ Dissolve the sugar in 300ml water and bring to just below boiling point. Remove from the heat, add the tea and leave, covered, in the pan to infuse for 3 hours.

♥ Strain into a freezer container, add the lemon juice and 4 of the mint leaves, snipped (with a pair of scissors) into very thin ribbons.

♥ Cover the container and put it in the freezer. When the mixture is frozen at the edges, but still softish in the middle (1–2 hours), pour it into a food processor and process at high speed until the mixture is smooth. (This breaks down the ice crystals that will have formed, resulting in a smooth sorbet. If you don't do this step – which could also be performed with a rotary beater or an electric 'wand' – the result will have a slushy, more granular effect, like an Italian granita.)

♥ Return to the freezer, and refreeze for several hours.

♥ Remove from the freezer about 30 minutes before serving and spoon the sorbet into glasses, or porcelain bowls, celadon-glazed for preference. Decorate each serving with a mint leaf sprinkled with water then dipped in sugar.

# macerated figs, apricots and prunes

These three fruits have two things in common. First, they promote regularity, and second (for those of us who live away from the places in which they are grown), figs, apricots and prunes are often better dried than when fresh.

The finest figs come either from California, where they were imported via Spain in 1880 by Mexican Franciscan monks, or from Izmir in Aegean Turkey. Californian Black Mission figs have a succulence all of their own. In their summer season they are fragrant and delicious – and make willing partners with wafer-thin slices of a cured ham such as *prosciutto di Parma*, or *jamón de Jabugo*.

Until 1923, Smyrna (modern Izmir) was a cosmopolitan, Greek-influenced enclave, a port that offered a window on Europe, and home to a thriving community of Greek, Armenian and Jewish traders. Smyrna figs may be green or yellow-tinged, or purple-skinned, and often have a powdery blush to their appearance. Fresh, they may not always have quite the luscious fragrance of their Black Mission cousins, but when sun-dried, they attain a seductive sensuality of taste and texture.

Figs from wherever have always been considered sexy. They are self-fertilizing, and their moist pink flower-seeded flesh symbolizes fecundity and carries an air of secrecy, with the lack of external fragrance offering no clue to their exotic, erotic inside. Sculptors have employed fig leaves as *caches-sexes* almost since Adam and Eve used them to hide their nakedness. As Jane Grigson, in her wonderful *Fruit Book* observes: 'That kind of role has clung to [the fig leaf], with patrons of art worrying about nudity. All right for them of course, but bad for the public – you and me – and shocking for the ladies. This has always puzzled me. We give birth and clean up the messes of infancy and illness; are we not strong enough to look at marble nudity? Were we not strong enough even in those messier days? Apparently not. Fig leaves were strapped on, round the galleries of the world, with elegant curves and exaggerations of size.'

While the downy, illicit promise of a fresh apricot may not always be fulfilled in terms of flavour, when dried the fruit becomes a powerhouse of sweet, saturated, sunny flavours. The very best dried apricots come either from the hills behind Adelaide, south Australia or the plains of Malatya, in south-east Turkey, both of which areas produce wonderfully fleshy fruit and enjoy the climate with which to sun-dry it. There are other varieties of apricot: the Hunza Valley in Afghanistan (Shangri-La of ancient repute) and orchards in the north of Iran produce a large-stoned fragrant apricot.

Incorporating Hunza apricots in a diet of yoghurt and simple grains was said to be the path to exceptional longevity. International and civil wars have meant that the outside world has been somewhat starved of good Hunza apricots over the last 20 years, although some foreign-grown examples are starting to surface again in Iranian and Indian grocery stores. Please do write in if, after eating them, you find yourself living for ever. However, Hunza apricots are not suitable for this recipe.

The lands of Asia Minor also produce sharp apricots. These are delicious – a dark colour, approaching tawny, and a tart yet non-astringent flavour. Sharp apricots (sometimes sold as 'leaf' apricots, as they are sliced from the stone before sun-drying, which causes them to curl like leaves) are for cooking with meat dishes – lamb and apricot *khoresh* (stew) mirrors the pre-Muhammadan duotheistic Ahura Mazda religion. Two gods, one good, one bad, one light, one dark, and so on. Two foods, the lamb sweetly savoury, the apricots sharply fruity, would be cooked together until they became balanced and harmonious. Sharp apricots are also delicious when reconstituted in sugared rose water, but, like their Hunza cousins, are not ideal here.

A perfectly- ripe plum, fresh off the tree, is an essay in contrasts. The skin, either blue-purple, sharp red, golden yellow or the green of a Reine-Claude, is smooth, blooming. This must be a suave, sophisticated fruit, you think. After all, it was named for Queen Claude, wife of François I. But bite into a ripe plum and it will show you its lustier nature. A hint of astringency, which seems to lie just under the skin, is overrun by a richly sugared taste and juicy, slightly fibrous flesh, which begs to be sucked and sucked until plum juice dribbles down your chin. Perhaps because fresh plums do not travel well, certain varieties are traditionally dried into prunes, a process that concentrates their flesh into a succulent, wrinkled delight, slightly resistant to the teeth.

Prunes may form the butt of geriatric jokes, but they are the serious eaters' good friend. Prunes from Agen, in south-west France, are considered the acme of prune civilization. Those sold half-dried (*mi-cuit*) have the most flavour and command the highest prices. In 1850, Agen plum rootstock was taken by a Frenchman, Louis Pellier, to California, where they now produce more prunes than anywhere else. Californian prunes are as good as anywhere else in the world, but can be rather over-preserved (with potassium sorbate), and thus require careful washing, if the results are not to be scummy.

The object of this recipe is to make all three macerations separately, thence to be enjoyed individually, or served as accessories to other dishes, or enjoyed as a glorious whole. For each fruit, I offer alcoholic and non-alcoholic versions, each of which is as good as the other. As each maceration takes time, it is well worth making large quantities of these conserves and enjoying them over a period of time. If you wish to store the conserves out of the fridge, preserve them in a liquid that is half light-sugar syrup and half the other designated liquid. Otherwise, keep the fruit in the refrigerator, turning the jar occasionally, for at least 1 month, and ideally until Christmas, whichever comes later.

## makes 72

**preparation about 1 hour, plus overnight soaking and macerating**

*for the figs*
**24 perfect dried figs**
**equal parts grape juice and Cointreau or orange blossom water**
**lemon and orange peel**

*for the apricots*
**24 perfect dried apricots**
**cinnamon quills**
**equal parts grape juice and gin or Ocean Spray cranberry juice**

*for the prunes*
**24 unsoaked stoned prunes (mi-cuit, though delicious, become too soft here; choose fully dried)**
**vanilla pods, split lengthwise**
**Pineau de Charentes, fino sherry or vervain tea**

*to serve*
**soft goats' cheese or crème fraîche and amaretto biscuits or warm toasted almonds, walnuts and pistachio kernels**

♥ To prepare the figs: soak them in just-boiled water for 1 hour, then drain. Add to the flavouring liquids, punctuating the jar with slivers of peel. Make sure that the fruit is completely covered by the liquid.

♥ Seal the jar, first with cling-film then with a lid.

♥ To prepare the apricots: plump them overnight in just-boiled water.

♥ Next day, drain the fruit and skewer them with the shards of cinnamon quill.

♥ Place upright in a jar and completely cover with the flavouring liquid. Seal as for the figs.

♥ To prepare the prunes: with a sharp knife or skewer, make a small hole through each prune.

♥ Skewer the prunes with pieces of the vanilla pods, place upright in a jar, and completely cover with the flavouring liquid. Seal as for the figs.

♥ Serve the fruits with soft goats' cheese or crème fraîche into which you've broken amaretto biscuits or with warm toasted almonds, walnuts and pistachio kernels.

# Machiko's sesame ice-cream

So fast, you'll have forgotten that you've had to make it. So delicious, your friends will bribe you for the recipe! Machiko Jinto (see also page 79) makes this beautiful dessert with Japanese black sesame paste. Worry not if you can't find this ingredient – most health and ethnic stores carry tahini, either whole (dark) or hulled (light). These Mediterranean pastes tend towards the oily – so for this recipe, use well-drained paste.

**500ml tub of your favourite vanilla ice-cream**
**2 tablespoons sesame paste**

♥ Allow the ice-cream to soften in the refrigerator, but not melt.
♥ Place it in a bowl with the sesame paste and slowly but surely beat the two together with a rotary mixer until one has become the other, and together they make one.
♥ Replace the ice-cream in the carton and freeze until firm.
♥ Remember to thank Machiko for so simply delicious a dessert!

# digestive tea with fennel and cardamom seeds

I pay great attention to the workings of my digestive system. So would you, if you too spent all day thinking about, writing on and playing with food. The urge to eat my food-fantasies-made-flesh can be overwhelming, but (I console myself) that is simply the price that must be paid for one's passion. 'But how,' I hear you asking yourselves, 'does he maintain so svelte a figure?' The answer, dear readers, lies between a happy home life, the awful realities embodied by the gym, and this delicious digestive tea.

The seat of disease is in our diet – all the great religions and any number of quacks say so – but surely God would not have sent us such alluring foods, and the knowledge of how to combine them into such great combinations as, say, cherries mashed with goats' cheese, if we weren't supposed to enjoy them! Those same religions that sell us the concept of original sin, and make Eve wrong for eating an apple, have a vested interest in maintaining our guilt levels. Without guilt, we wouldn't need to go church or temple, because we wouldn't feel guilty for missing it. And without guilt, we'd see a passionate love of food simply for what it is – an enthusiastic response to gifts granted by our Creator.

For those of us who have neither the time, the training nor the discipline to refuse food before the previous meal has been completely digested, I offer this excellent digestive tea (which can be made in advance and kept for up to a month).

**makes enough for about 20 cups of tea**

**preparation about 30 minutes, plus cooling**

5 tablespoons cardamom pods
5 tablespoons fennel seeds
2 teaspoons coarse sea salt
Angostura bitters

♥ Toast the cardamom pods in a hot dry frying pan, until they start to snap, crackle and pop. Remove from the pan and leave to cool.

♥ Toast the fennel seeds in the same manner, removing them as soon as they start to release their aniseed fragrance.

♥ Crack the cardamom pods with your fingers and remove the seeds, discarding the pods. Mix the fennel and cardamom seeds with the salt and crush gently. Try to achieve a very coarse mixture.

♥ Store in an airtight jar in a cool, dark place.

♥ To serve, add a teaspoon of the mixture to a cup of freshly boiled water. Add a good dash (about 7 drops) of Angostura bitters and cover the cup. Leave for up to 15 minutes and then sip the tea, trying not to think too hard about what's for supper.

# chapter seven
## feasting

If the car is the biggest thing you can wear, then the feast is the biggest thing you can eat. Feasting celebrates all that this book is about: there would be no food were it not for the farmers and fishermen who produce it on our behalf, hence feasting honours them, as much as it respects and glorifies the seasons. And when it comes to preparing the feast, the sense of abundance displayed in food stores is intended to ignite in us a similar spirit of abandon, encouraging us to offer to the table more than mere sustenance, but also a feast for the senses.

Even the simplest of foods becomes a feast when the cook's intention is strong and pure. This theory works for groups and individuals, too: by following the practice of Kitchen Yoga, a simple supper for one becomes a spiritual feast. Families and friends too deserve to be feted by food, and a feast is the best remedy for relationship fatigue, when its atmosphere of the extraordinary serves to remind us just what it was that we first found so special in our loved ones. Lovers deserve the feast treatment as well, for the feast intends for us to sate our appetites.

On the subject of sated appetites, here's my interpretation of *The Barmecide Feast*, a favourite story from Arabian Nights: Harun el Rashid, the fabled Caliph of Baghdad, had a wise and just vizier, known as the Barmecide, whose home was a beautiful palace in the midst of flower-filled gardens. In the same land there was a poor man called Shac'abac, a penniless, yet optimistic mendicant, whose hunger one day got the better of him. I'll visit the Barmecide,' thought he: 'I can feast on his leftovers.'

A servant led our rag-clad dervish through ever-grander audience chambers to the dining hall where, at the end of a long empty table sat the Barmecide, finely-robed, white-bearded, shrewd-eyed. Shac'abac bowed and recited his troubles. 'Is it possible?' demanded the grand but kindly vizier. 'Look at you! You must be half-dead with hunger. I have more than enough food for you and for all of Baghdad – let us feast together!' He turned and hailed a servant: 'Boy! Bring us water scented with orange blossom to wash with, and instruct the cook to hurry supper, we have a guest!'

Shac'abac, nonplussed, protested in the formulaic way of the east, but his Lord would have none of it: 'Come wash with me!' he commanded, rinsing his elegant fingers in an imaginary stream of scented water, poured by an invisible servant. What to do?  If Shac'abac played along, would he be exposed as a flatterer. And questioning a powerful vizier's motives would be tantamount to a death sentence. Unwilling to be made fun of, as even a mendicant has some vestigial pride, and fearful for his life, he had no recourse other than to trust his master, on whose charity he depended. So he washed his hands enthusiastically, even complementing the Barmecide on the temperature of his water.

'Let us eat! commanded the Barmecide, 'You said you're hungry, so eat your fill – have you tried roast suckling pig? Even though it's forbidden?! Come, let me carve for you!' Shac'abac – confused, tantalized – agreed that he indeed secretly loved young pork. 'What do you like most about it?' demanded the vizier: 'the melting soft pale flesh?' By now half out of his mind and faint with hunger but unwilling to appear greedy, Shac'abac groaned that it might the crisp crackle of the skin he preferred. 'Then let us enjoy its savoury chew...!'

At this point, our Moslem friends would have us believe that Shac'abac passed the test by refusing make-believe wine, upon which the real feast was served in reward. Jews and Catholics alike will understand poor Shac'abac's guilt, and Buddhists find solace in the concept of thirst quenched from an empty cup. Those of us who went to bed with Hans Christian Anderson will remember the Emperor's new clothes, and (hopefully) the value of truth in all things. No matter your beliefs, I wish you many guilt-free, fun-filled, recklessly abandoned feasts!

# morels stuffed with potato and Taleggio

serves 4

**preparation 30 minutes**

16 or 20 large fresh morels, or dried
morels reconstituted in cold water
150g young Taleggio cheese
1 medium potato, mashed
4 tablespoons good olive oil
freshly ground black pepper

*A turkey baster or needleless syringe is
essential here to pipe the mixture into
the mushrooms.*

♥ Preheat the oven to 180°C.

♥ Bring a pan of water to the boil, and drop in the morels (if using dried, boil in soaking water for 3 minutes after reconstitution). Remove the mushrooms and reserve the liquor.

♥ Fork the Taleggio into the mashed potato, adding as much of the liquor as needed to achieve a smooth mixture.

♥ Pipe the mixture into the morels and place snugly into an ovenproof dish. Pour over 100ml of the soaking liquor (or stock, if you haven't enough liquor) and the oil, then sprinkle with pepper. Bake for 10-15 minutes, until the cheese bubbles.

♥ Serve as a starter or supper dish, or to accompany a great piece of meat, such as No-salt Massaged Shoulder of Lamb (page 66).

# buttered baby spinach

There's a certain luxury in using the youngest, most innocent spinach for this dish. Older leaves work just as well, but can't deliver quite the same chaste yet glamorous flavour as baby spinach.

serves 4 as an
accompaniment

**preparation 15 minutes**

250g very young, very green spinach
2 tablespoons unsalted butter
1 garlic clove, crushed with the flat
of a knife
sea salt and white pepper (optional)

♥ Wash all the leaves and shake them dry - there is no need to remove stalks unless you are dealing with older leaves.
♥ Place in a large heavy-bottomed pan that has a tight-fitting lid with the butter, garlic and a sprinkling of salt. Cover and cook on the lowest possible heat for about 10 minutes. Give the contents a stir. You can judge at this point how long (if at all) to carry on cooking (unlikely to be more than another 5 minutes).
♥ Taste and adjust the seasoning, finishing with a little white pepper if you wish, and not forgetting to fish out the garlic.

# potatoes mashed with truffles

Truffles are impossible to cultivate and delicious to eat. These tiny fungi are found by specially trained dogs (or hogs - to which truffles smell like sow-on-heat) in forests where they lie buried under piles of rotting leaves. Truffles are found all over the world, but are most enthusiastically traded in France and Italy, where the cuisines venerate them. There are different varieties: unscrupulous stores and restaurateurs use this confusion to overcharge wildly.

Broadly speaking, the best to buy are *Tuber Melanosporum*: jet black on the outside (known as the black diamond of the forest, in fact) brown on the inside, and with an unmistakable aroma that should remind you of, well, sex. There, I've said it. *T. Melanosporum* is sold as both Winter and Summer truffle; when eaten, even in tiny quantities, the memory of its sensual flavour lingers on the breath for many hours.

*Tuber Aestivum* is sold only as Summer truffle. When ripe, its skin is black, albeit a lighter colour than *T. Melanosporum*, and mottled to boot. *T. Aestivum* is practically tasteless - avoid it.

*Tuber Magnatum* and *Tuber Borchii* are very similar - both are cream or light brown in colour, and similarly pale when cut. Both exhibit some of the sexy aroma and taste of *T. Melanosporum*, but without the same satisfying intensity. Not to be summarily dismissed, they come a reasonable second to *T. Melanosporum* black diamonds. In my book, the word for this truffle's tantalizing, titillating aroma is evanescent.

As I mentioned, so far truffles have proved to be impossible to cultivate, and truffle traders are making great capital of the fungus's rarity. It's true that harvests are diminishing, and it is in the trader's interest to under-report them. Truffles thrive in Southern European forests where hornbeam, oak and hazel trees grow. Deforestation (for roads, housing, olive trees, etc.) has meant that the truffle has a declining habitat, although the French traders of Périgord, and the Italians of Alba now have a worldwide scouting system, which means that the truffles you buy may as easily have come from North Africa or South America as from Southern Europe.

A last word on how and what to buy. Fresh truffles are sold at room temperature, under glass and by weight. They cost plenty. A very reliable source is La Maison de la Truffe (www.maison-de-la-truffe.com) in Place de la Madeleine, Paris. Fresh truffles can easily be kept at home - pop one in a plastic bag with some eggs for a day or two, and your eggs will be imbued with truffle. Equally, a truffle buried in rice will last for a few weeks, and the rice will become exquisitely fragranced. Fresh truffles should not, in my opinion, be cooked. Simply shave them on to your finished dish (see my very easy recipe below) and eat immediately. Truffle mandolins exist for the enthusiast - a very sharp knife and a steady hand will do almost as well.

Truffles that are sold preserved in pretty jars, either in oil or in 'juice' are not worth it - aroma and smell are minimal, even though they tend to be expensive. Good-quality truffle oil, on the other hand, is a boon in the kitchen, when used sparingly to add panache and élan to pasta, rice and egg dishes.

Best budget bet is truffle paste, which is usually inexpensive, and should deliver some real truffle flavour. Look out for paste with *T. Melanosporum*, which should be preserved in olive oil and (usually) wild mushroom paste, which makes a very superior spread on buttered toast.

To make potatoes mashed with much butter and truffles: first mash your potatoes - the trick is to incorporate as much air and butter and cream into the mixture as you can. When you've achieved a smooth mash, shave as much truffle as you own over the top and serve. That's it!

# caviar with dill blinis and lemon vodka

Caviar is the cocaine of the food world: it is an acquired taste, disappears in a trice and is a mad extravagance. Only the roe of the sturgeon may properly be called caviar, and the only sturgeon that matter live in the Caspian Sea. (Although valiant efforts are being made in California and Acquitaine, France to farm the fish in the face of wild over-fishing by some deregulated Russian fishermen who cater to a burgeoning home market of newly-rich 'businessmen'.) The Caspian being a large lake rather than a sea, Caspian sturgeon are the unmutated descendants of 3-million-year-old dinosaur fish which swam within its shores, hardly altered by the evolutionary process.

Like salmon, the sturgeon returns to its birthplace to spawn, swimming up the Volga and Ural deltas at Spring and Autumn equinox. For many centuries, the Russian, Iranian, Azeri, Turkmeni and Kazakh fishermen who harvest this fish were the only eaters of the sturgeon's eggs, which were considered gauche next to the delicacy of its flesh. The Roman Emperor Severus, for example, served sturgeon at banquets, resplendent on a bed of rose petals, fêted with flutes and drums.

Much later, the Petrossian brothers, who were Armenian Russians fleeing the Bolsheviks, introduced the Tsarist taste for caviar to 1920s Paris. Until the break-up of the Soviet Union, nearly all caviar was marketed from there, but the anarchic chaos that has ensued in the pursuit of democracy means that the eggs in your lapis lazuli bowl will now be from Iran: an irony as the sturgeon is not considered halal.

The most prized of all sturgeon is the Beluga, the roe of which is the largest, pale or dark-grey in colour and with a subtly iodized tang to it. Beluga can easily live to 100 years or more, and a good specimen weighs a tonne. Next in scale is the Oscietra, a mere 60 years at maturity, which grows to around 300kg, and whose glamorous roe has a golden sheen; followed by Sevruga, a relative baby at 20 years and 60 kilos. Sevruga eggs have a small inky-black grain, and the most vivid flavour of all caviar.

A stressed sturgeon delivers spoilt eggs, so specially-trained 'captains' dispatch the fish silently with a swift slash to the gills. These master surgeons then immediately remove the egg sac by Caesarian section. The roe is graded, salted, then matured before sale. Malossol (lightly salted) denotes fresh perfect eggs whose taste requires little masking, unlike pressed caviar, which is made from the roe of more than one fish, whose eggs may have been crushed or broken, and thus require heavier salting.

Tasting caviar requires a spoon of horn, mother-of-pearl, amber or gold (steel spoils the flavour, plastic is fine, and may even be ironic, considering the price of caviar), and a draught of vodka to mollify the eggs' intense oiliness. Those that know say that caviar should never be swallowed, but crushed frivolously against the roof of the mouth. It should never be snorted, although its price is not to be sniffed at, and one should be content with merely paying for it through the nose.

The idea of eating caviar with chopped onion and all that stuff was only introduced to mask the taste of off eggs. Therefore, all you need is:

### serves 4

**preparation 20 minutes, plus 2½-3 hours' standing**

**as much caviar as you can afford (there are also good black herring and lumpfish roe which, though lacking caviar's delicacy, may fool guests)**
**sour cream or crème fraîche, to serve**
**lemon vodka, to serve**

*for the blinis (adapted from Linda Collister's The Bread Book, makes 12 small light yeasty blinis*
**1 packet (15g) of dried yeast, or 15g of fresh**
**1 teaspoon sugar**
**170ml lukewarm water**
**1 small egg separated**
**140g buckwheat flour (or equal parts buckwheat and plain flour)**
**1 teaspoon salt**
**170ml lukewarm milk**
**2 tablespoons finely chopped dill, plus more whole sprigs for garnish**
**a knob of butter, for frying**

♥ Mix the yeast and sugar, then whisk in the water.

♥ Whisk the egg yolk and add to the flour. Mix in the yeast mixture and the salt to make a thick batter.

♥ Cover with a damp tea towel until doubled in volume (1½-2 hours).

♥ Beat the milk into the mixture, then cover again until bubbles appear on the surface (around 1 hour).

♥ Whisk the egg white until quite stiff, then fold it into the batter with the dill.

♥ Heat a buttered non-stick frying pan to medium-hot, then ladle in small pools of the mixture and cook in batches for 2-3 minutes each. Turn the blinis over with a palette knife, and cook for a couple of minutes more. Repeat until all the batter is used.

♥ Serve warm, the soft yielding texture of the herbed blinis in contrast to the oily chill of the caviar and the sharp surprise of the iced lemon vodka. Garnish with a sprig of fresh dill, if you're feeling up to it, and maybe a dollop or two of sour cream or crème fraîche. Take the phone off the hook and attack the vodka before it attacks you.

*Lemon vodka. I recommend a quality brand, such as Polish Wyborowka, the crystal-clear flavour and subtle lemon fragrance of which enhances the taste of both the caviar and the blinis.*

# Maine lobster with beurre blanc

Maine is Vacationland for the millions of Americans who visit each year, but for lobsters it's Grand Central Station. Nowhere else in the world fishes as many of them, or manages to maintain quality standards so successfully. Stringent conservation criteria mean that yields of the crustacea are at record levels (57 million pounds weight last year) and rising, thus bringing prosperity for the boats and dealers, and the taste of luxury to ever more tables.

Ogunquit is a postcard-pretty Maine fishing and holiday town. By seven in the morning, the Perkins Cove parking lot is full of brand-new pickup trucks, loaded up with lobster pots. The talk is of Bush and Gorbachev - not their politics, but their eating policy. Recently the elder Bush had come down from neighbouring Kennebunkport with the last leader of the Soviets for a real Maine lobster supper, bibs and claws and corn and all. Two Presidents together, eating the king of seafood. Were they, we wonder, cracking voter jokes whilst cracking claws?

Ogunquit fisherman Eric Brazer is blasé on the subject: 'We've gotten used to Presidential visits over the years,' he says, 'It's nice that they come, but we have our own fish to fry.' At 53, Eric is one of the older men still out fishing lobster daily, albeit with some younger muscle to help him lift traps. 'There's a State-sponsored apprentice programme, designed to maintain safety and quality standards as much as to prevent over-fishing,' he says, 'And young people can only fish by taking that course, then waiting for someone to retire.' Eric has friends of his own age who are taking up golf, but his frank blue eyes admit a love for this sea life that make his retirement a dim prospect yet.

State wardens are out on the water at all times, checking permits, boats and catches. Eric insists that they are welcome: 'The lesson we've learned,' he says, 'Is that by taking care of our stocks, we're guaranteeing ourselves a good living in the future.' Maine imposes a limit of 800 traps per boat, then (taking advice from university marine scientists) caps the number of boat permits. Lobsters were traditionally fished when 7 years old, but 4 years back, Maine legislated for a new minimum catch size - the permissible distance from eye socket to first tail ridge was increased from 3 to 31/4 inches – making the taking of 8-year-old specimens the norm. Any boat found catching a 'short' loses its permit, it's as simple as that. Breeding stocks are similarly protected. If trapped pregnant females ('eggers') have notches cut into their tails – possession of an egger loses you your licence the same way.

All this makes sound economic sense to Eric. 'For every egger that stays in the water another year, that's 5,000 more eggs she can produce. Mind you, not all of those eggs survive.' Nature has a perfect way with lobster eggs. When hatched, they float to the surface, where they stay for a week. Those that aren't eaten by birds or washed to the shore scatter and sink - if the eggs stayed in one area, there simply wouldn't be enough food for them all to eat. In the water, older lobsters have their predators too: cod, wolf fish, seal and striped bass all love a lobster supper, and herein, suggests Eric, lies another explanation for the proliferation of the Maine lobster.

'About 10 to 15 years ago, the trawler-men (with new sonar equipment) decimated inshore cod stocks. Cod eat lobster, so no cod equals more lobster.' Eric also has reason to thank the Japanese affection for seafood. 'In the last 5 years, we experienced a huge demand from Japan for sea urchin roe, although,' he laughs, 'You wouldn't catch me eating that stuff myself!' Eric's theory is simple and perfect: sea urchins feed on seaweed and kelp. Eliminate all the sea urchins by over-diving them and the sea vegetables re-grow, adding another rich source of food for the lobsters.

In May, June and July, Maine fishermen throw back about 80% of their catch. This is the egging and moulting season, and new-shell specimens are too weak to withstand much travelling. New-shell lobster gets shipped to restaurants without saltwater holding tanks, for immediate consumption. In Ogunquit, by the first week in August, the new shells are hardy enough to last a few days in Perkins Cove. Eric explains: 'We keep them in the Cove in pots of 100 for up to 3 days, but then have to move them on to a dealer - otherwise the lobster eat each other. The harbour temperature is 65°F, but the dealer keeps the lobsters in refrigerated tanks, at 46°F. This kind of rejuvenates them, hardens up their shells, sort of stabilizes them ready for transport.'

By October, the lobster season is in full swing, although most Maine boats fish all year round, weather permitting. Autumn means lobster for dinner in the Brazer household, and Eric professes a taste for male lobsters, demonstrating how to differentiate between the sexes: the side swimmerets on males are long, sharp and shiny, whereas females sport pretty feathery ones. And the female tail is broader (and therefore more sought after by the processors who deal in frozen tail meat), whilst the male's somewhat slimmer back also means bigger, meatier claws.

The State of Maine should be commended for its effort and forward-thinking, as are the fishermen who abide by State regulations. Smart marketing of Maine lobster has meant that customer demand has risen to coincide with the increased harvests occasioned by this conservation-minded approach to fishing. This, in turn, has meant that wholesale and retail prices have stayed steady, resulting in sustained profit margins for the boats and the dealers, while wages inflation means that the lobster in the shops is now actually more affordable than ever. Lobster is no longer the preserve of presidents, but simply the taste of guilt-free luxury.

While most of Maine serves boiled lobster, with dips and a cob of corn, I find the Normandy manner of serving it even more delicious:

serves 2

**preparation about 30 minutes**

1 large lobster (around 1½ lb) or 2 smaller ones
140g unsalted butter
1 small shallot, very finely chopped
4 tablespoons white wine vinegar or dry white wine
salt

♥ Preheat the oven to 190ºC.
If your lobster is already cooked, simply reheat it in the hot oven, with a little butter rubbed on the shell for shine. If not, kill your lobster with a sharp knife straight through the little cross in the centre of the head, then cut through the entire length of the body. Remove the intestinal thread which runs down the tail, and the small sac which lies in the top of the head.

♥ Over a medium-low heat, melt a large knob from the butter in a sauté pan large enough to accommodate both (all) the lobster halves.

♥ When the butter has stopped foaming, place the lobster pieces in the pan, cut side down, and gently sauté for 10–15 minutes (10 for small lobster, up to 15 for big ones). Turn once, towards the end of the cooking, by which time the shells should have turned red.

♥ Keep the cooked lobster warm in the bottom of the oven, while you make the beurre blanc: in a saucepan over a moderate heat, cook the shallot in the vinegar or wine until very soft.

♥ Add the butter, a spoonful at a time, whisking it mercilessly to keep it emulsified. Add as much of the butter as you feel comfortable with, but don't forget to whisk unceasingly. Taste the beurre blanc and add salt to taste

♥ Serve immediately in bowls to accompany the lobster.

# roasted brill with scallops, potatoes, chestnuts and endive

Michelin-starred restaurants offer a certain style of eating, thought to be especially luxurious. To me, the places that have earned their stars often offer a certain period glamour – you know, the stately service, the chimera waiters anticipating your every brain wave, appearing before your table as if blessed with second sight. (Or, as Woody Allen once said, and Yogi Berra before him – 'Like déjà vu all over again!')

If restaurants were chairs, the ones that get the stars would be Louis Quattorze numbers, intricately carved, beautiful to look at, made of fine materials, but (he whispered) perhaps not all that comfortable to sit on. There are times, let's face it, that we'd much rather be eating the equivalent of a bean bag, or a Tom Dixon chair, or a Joe Columbo sofa, for that matter. Actually, food thought worthy of Michelin stars tends toward the over-manipulated, as if, in an echo of late 19th-century mores, Man had overcome Nature's imperfections, and taught it a damned good lesson in the kitchen by forcing ingredients into shapes, textures and flavours other than their natural ones.

In the days when this style of eating was considered luxurious, only a small élite travelled out of their towns, the rest of us being doomed to stay put, eating a diet based on the same few ingredients during each season. But now! Ta ra! Travel is cheap and available, and true luxury involves simpler, rarer pleasures, such as perfectly fresh, untainted, unmanipulated ingredients to eat, as well as the time and space in which to enjoy them. However, there is still a place for old-fashioned gastronomy: de luxe food speaks to a certain constituency, most usually those whose digestion has been trained to eat rich food over many years, or those who equate money with quality (known in the restaurant trade as gastro-gnomes, and always relied on to spend top dollar on the worst wines on the list).

In saying that, there's a certain occasional pleasure to be had in sampling flashy gastronomy, particularly when there's a chef with a special touch, (or when somebody else is picking up the tab). Most young chefs aim for the stars by way of competing with their contemporaries - there's a school of thought that suggests that, in any case, chefs cook their food for the benefit of other chefs as much as to please their customers – and Michelin-style food is designed to impress the restaurant critic first, in an effort to bring in the high rollers. So there you have it, the problems suffered by this approach to luxury dining is that the chef's passion is necessarily subsumed by the need to impress – extrovert flavours are considered incompatible with an educated palate, and other such tosh.

However, risking hypocrisy (not for the first time, nor the last ),
I offer here a recipe from a 30-something-year-old Michelin-starred French chef
called Christophe Moisand, who cooks at Le Celadon Restaurant at the Hôtel
Westminster in Paris, along the Rue Daunou from Harry's Bar. Christophe is an
impressive character, with an even, steady temperament, and a gift for sharing
his knowledge with his adoring young brigade. I include his dish because a) it's
delicious, b) I like chestnuts, c) I like endives (and brill, scallops and potatoes) and
d) because devoted young chefs like Christophe deserve our plaudits and
encouragement just as Michelin restaurant inspectors need a kick up the rear to
hoist them into the 20th, let alone the 21st century.

I have adapted this recipe to make it easily achievable for those of you
who don't have a brigade of 15 to support you at home.

### serves 4

**preparation about 40 minutes**

225g salad potatoes (Christophe uses la ratte), peeled
150g unsalted butter
coarse sea salt
365g scallop meat (or a mixture of other shelled seafood)
8 peeled cooked chestnuts from a vacuum pack or a jar
about 1 cup of fish stock (reserved from the scallops, if you've opened them yourself)
4 slices of brill, each about 250g
2 heads of white endive, leaves separated
100ml crème fraîche (optional)

♥ Pan-roast the potatoes in half of the butter in a covered pan, adding salt to season, and adding the scallops (or other seafood) 2 minutes before the potatoes are done.

♥ Meanwhile, heat the chestnuts in the fish or scallop stock.

♥ Over a medium heat, fry the fish in the rest of the butter, skin side down first, turning once after 2 minutes.

♥ After turning the fish, add the endive to the pan. Remove both after 2 minutes and keep warm.

♥ Drain the chestnuts, adding their cooking stock to deglaze the fish pan.

♥ Add the cream, if using it, and the drained chestnuts to the deglazed pan and heat to reduce it a little, but take care not to allow it to boil.

♥ Serve the brill and endives surrounded by the butter-roasted potatoes and scallops, and the creamy chestnuts.

# porcini-stuffed poussins

Dried porcini add their woodsy fragrance to these young birds, and they accent the subtle flavour of fresh porcini. Encourage guests to devour these delicious baby chickens with their fingers!

serves 4

**preparation about 2 hours**

4 garlic cloves, thinly sliced
a little vegetable or light olive oil
100g fresh field or wild porcini mushrooms, roughly chopped
20g dried porcini, soaked for 15 minutes in a cup of hot water, soaking water reserved
coarse salt and freshly ground pepper
8 tablespoons toasted breadcrumbs
4 poussins
2 glasses of white wine

*Have ready finger bowls of warm water with a slice of lemon and a good dash of orange blossom water, and slave boys or girls to wash and massage your feet.*

♥  Preheat the oven to 230°C. Sauté the garlic in the oil until just coloured. Remove from the pan and reserve.

♥  In the same oil over a gentle heat, sauté the chopped fresh mushrooms until they start to give up their juice. Add the chopped soaked dried mushrooms and stir well. The mixture should be moist; if too dry, add some dried mushroom soaking juices. Season well.

♥  Remove from the heat and stir in about half of the garlic with enough of the breadcrumbs to make a stiff filling.

♥  Working your finger under the skin of each poussin, secrete a few slices of the remaining garlic around the breasts and in their armpits.

♥  Stuff the birds with the mushroom mixture and sew or skewer up the openings (any leftover stuffing can be rolled in foil and baked at the bottom of the oven, at the same time as the birds).

♥  Sprinkle the birds all over with salt and sit them, breast down, in a large roasting tin into which you've poured the wine. Put the birds in the oven, immediately reducing the heat to 180°C. Cook for 20 minutes, then turn the birds over on their backs, sprinkle the breasts with coarse salt and cook for a further 20 minutes, basting once.

♥  Remove from the oven and let rest for 10 minutes, during which time you may reduce the cooking juices to about half their volume.

♥  Serve with the juices on the side, to be eaten with the fingers.

# roast goose, foie gras, fried apples, lemon verbena

Roast goose has a lovely rich flavour. In the Northern Hemisphere, geese for eating tend to hatch from around Easter, being therefore ready to eat between Michaelmas and Christmas. This recipe is, therefore, a cold-weather feast dish, made wholly indulgent by the addition of fattened goose liver.

For those who are concerned about such things, the making of foie gras, (as introduced to the Romans by the Jews of South East France) comprises surprisingly little 'cruelty' to the goose. In order to introduce into a goose the huge amounts of corn required to distend the liver, the bird must be completely at its ease. Geese for foie gras, therefore, almost always have a close relationship with their feeders, becoming agitated and refusing food, for instance, if their feeder changes. Does this mean that these birds implicitly agree to their fat fate? Ask your priest, or your therapist, if you must, but remember that food guilt is probably as much of a sin as any other. (Do not ask this type of advice of your personal trainer; you'll only be made to suffer!)

If possible, buy a goose that's already been boned, as it makes an easier package to deal with than an unboned bird. And, when roasted, geese give up lots of wonderful fat (excellent for roast potatoes!).

## serves 6 or more (depending on the size of your goose)

**preparation 3-4 hours**

1 goose
3 or 4 hard apples
2 tablespoons lemon juice
2 tablespoons dried lemon verbena leaves
2 tablespoons hot water
3 or 4 potatoes, peeled, sliced and parboiled
sea salt and freshly ground black pepper
½ bottle of Gewürztraminer or other

♥ Preheat the oven to 190°C. Weigh your bird and then calculate cooking time at 44 minutes per kg. Prick the skin all over to encourage the fat to run.

♥ Peel and core the apples, then slice them and soak the slices in the lemon juice to prevent discoloration. Reconstitute the dried lemon verbena leaves in the hot water for 5 minutes.

♥ Season the parboiled potatoes, add the lemon verbena leaves, then stuff inside the bird. Seal up the cavity with string or skewers.

♥ Pour the wine into the roasting dish, then place the bird in the dish and season all over generously with salt and pepper. Roast, turning and basting the bird every 20 minutes. Halfway through cooking, lower the oven setting to 180°C.

♥ About 10 minutes before the time that you've calculated cooking

**Alsace wine**
**a large knob of butter, plus more**
**for greasing**
**a cup of ice cubes**
**as much foie gras as you can**
**afford, cleaned and cut into ½**
**cm slices**

will be finished, splash cold water on the breast, then return to the heat. This encourages a crisp skin.

♥ Test for doneness by inserting a skewer into the meatiest part of the bird. If the juices run clear, you're OK. If not, carry on cooking. If you're concerned about the skin burning, cover it with some buttered greaseproof paper. Allow the cooked bird to rest for 20 minutes in a warm place before you carve it.

♥ Meanwhile, drain off all the lovely juices from the roasting tin into a jug, and add the ice cubes. Stir well for about a minute, during which time, some of the fat will coagulate around them, then remove them to a bowl, in order to decant the fat later (alternatively, siphon off carefully from the top with a bulb baster or pour into a fat separating jug). Ladle and skim off as much fat from the jug as you can.

♥ Just before serving, in a non-stick frying pan over a medium heat, melt the butter until it stops foaming. Add the drained apples and sauté for 1 minute, then season with plenty of pepper. Arrange around the bird.

♥ In the same pan, again over a medium heat, sear the slices of foie gras for about 15 seconds each side. Add to the apple arrangement and serve immediately, accompanied by the reheated roasted juices and the fragrant stuffing.

# Segovian suckling pig

A Castillian cochinillo is fed exclusively on its mother's milk. The pig is traditionally cooked in a walled wood-burning oven, and served whole on a large earthenware platter. This is not a dish for the timid as, though undeniably delicious to eat, a suckling pig looks awfully cute in death.

serves 8-10

**preparation about 3¼ hours**

1 suckling pig, weighing up to 7 kg
coarse salt
a few sprigs of fresh thyme
juice of 1 lemon
1 head of garlic, cloves separated and unpeeled

♥  Preheat the oven to 230°C. Score the pig's skin as you would for crackling and rub the cavity with a little coarse salt. Lay in a baking tray and add half a cup of water, thyme, lemon juice and garlic.

♥  Place, uncovered, in the hot oven and cook for 20 minutes, basting twice with the cooking juices.

♥  Lower the oven setting to 180°C and continue to cook for about 1 hour 40 minutes, basting enthusiastically for the first hour, but not at all after that. When done, the skin should be golden crispy, and a skewer should come out clean.

*for the accompaniments*
**1.5 kg new potatoes**
**2 tablespoons baby capers**
**2 tablespoons black olive paste**
**2 tablespoons finely chopped**
**gherkins**
**1 teaspoon grated lemon zest**

♥ Remove to a carving board and allow to rest for about 15 minutes before carving.

♥ While the pig cooks, prepare the potatoes, by first boiling them in salted water for 5 minutes. Drain and, when cool enough to handle, slice off and reserve the tops of each. With a teaspoon, scoop out some of the flesh, taking care to leave the walls intact.

♥ Mix the capers, olive paste, gherkins and lemon zest with enough potato flesh to make a thick mixture. Moisten with the meat's cooking juices, and spoon back into the potatoes. Replace the 'lids' and place on a tray at the bottom of the oven for about 40 minutes until nicely coloured. Alternatively, you can simply serve with plain roasted new potatoes, and the stuffing mixture on the side.

# honeyed raclette from the salamander

You could use any good melting cheese for this dish, a young Pecorino, perhaps, or a mild Cheddar, but to me, this is a dish made for raclette. This semi-hard cheese was purportedly discovered by alpine herders, who placed their frozen cheese next to a fire, scraped off the melted bits, and ate them over potatoes. Raclette is only ever eaten hot, and there are any number of raclette heaters available for the enthusiast.

For this treatment, the method is simple: take a heatproof oven dish and get it very hot, either in the oven, under a salamander (eye-level grill), or on the hob. When it's very hot, place a ½–1cm slice of raclette in the dish. It will bubble and hiss straight away. Pour a tablespoon of good honey (I like chestnut - its flavour stands up well next to the strong cheese) all over the surface, then slide the dish under the preheated grill. As soon as the cheese starts to bubble, remove from the grill and serve the soft, warm honeyed cheese straight from the oven dish, immediately. Stunning.

Thinking about honey, have you though recently about just how amazing is the bee? The bee is too often overlooked as an essential actor in nature's great play, especially as man falls into the trap (as he did 100 years ago) of fancying himself as better than creation, what with GM crops, and so on. Science is fallible, so perhaps a reminder of Albert Einstein's observation is timely: 'If the bee disappeared from the face of the Earth, Man would not last more than 4 years… no more bees, no more pollination, no more flora, no more animals. No more man.'

# strawberries with vincotto

Vincotto looks similar to balsamic vinegar, but has the opposite taste. While *balsamico* is sour and sweet, vincotto is sweet and a little sour (if you get my drift). My favourite vincotto is produced by the Calogiuri family in Lecce, near Salento, in Southern Italy and has been since 1825. The family's secret recipe, doubtless whispered into the ear of the eldest son of each generation, calls for the grape must to be cooked. The Calogiuris only use Negroamaro and Malvasia Nera grapes, which have been left to wither on the vine for 30 days. Cooked down to half its original volume, the must is then filtered and held in oak barrels for 4 years, during which time the more religious members of the Calogiuri clan probably recite their catechisms in the maturing room.

Whatever the niceties, the resulting vincotto is rich in healthy polyphenols and is thick but not syrupy, complex but not cloying. A few drops point up the flavours of both sweet and savoury dishes. I particularly love vincotto with strawberries. It's better than good with vanilla ice-cream, and adds excitement and sophistication when dripped into fruit Martinis.

Allow about 150g of washed strawberries per person. Larger fruit should be hulled, very sour fruit should be sugared and left at room temperature for an hour or so. Pile the fruit into a slim glass, and gently pour about half a teaspoon of vincotto over it. Serve at room temperature, straight away. www.vincotto.com

# arabic coffee

I love Arabic coffee. As a ritual, it is more satisfying than the on-the-hoof shot of espresso, and as a taste I find it infinitely more pleasing. Not that espresso per se is unpleasant, but simply that most espresso (out of Italy, at any rate) is badly made, and there's only so much bitter, astringent, over-extracted, burnt-bean, nerve-jangling punishment that a body can take.

Arabic (also known as Greek or Turkish) coffee has evolved little since it was discovered by a shepherd in Ethiopia, where some of the world's best coffee beans, including the chocolatey Mocha, come from. It involves no equipment save a small-necked, long-handled, funnel-shaped pan, and a flame. The pan, known as an *ibrik*, or a *tanaka*, may be of plain enamel or of beaten brass, but ensure the inside is Teflon-coated, as this makes for more *wesh* (see below). *Ibriks* come in varying sizes, from 2 to 8 cups, and Arabic coffee is offered unsweetened (*murra*), medium-sweet (*mazbout*), or very sweet (*helou*).

Using the small cup size into which you'll serve your coffee, measure about ¾ of a cup of water per person. Add sugar (if you're not helou enough already): a teaspoon per person for mazbout, double that for sweet, and bring to the boil.

Take a very heaped teaspoon of pulverized coffee per person, and add it to the boiling water. Stir it well, and bring back to the boil. When the mixture boils again (and take care, as it rises quickly up the sides of the tanaka), remove it from the heat, stir once and bring it back to the boil. At this point in the method, accounts vary as to the correct way to proceed. There are those that like to knock the ibrik against the side of the stove once, then to boil again and serve. Others knock three times and serve straight away. I've known people boil seven times and never knock! My grandmother would be scandalized. The best thing is to create your own ritual, trying absolutely your best to remain conscious of your coffee and your guest throughout. When pouring the coffee, remember the wesh. This is the froth without which no Arabic coffee is properly topped. Wesh is created in the boiling and knocking, and dispensed by making the hand tremble as the coffee is poured.

In certain circles, the convention is to finish one's coffee in exactly 3 slurps, though in my experience this leads to a burnt mouth. Better, if possible, is to take one's time - and to take care not to take in the coffee 'sludge' at the bottom of the cup, which is used only for inverting into the saucer for the predicting of fortunes. No, wait - I can see it clearly...

## thank you!

All these people gave of themselves to enable this book to be written. They helped with reckless abandon!

**A**
Munir and Oya Akdogan for their pure friendship
Michael Alcock my intelligent literary agent

**B**
Beachmere Inn at Ogunquit, Maine
Boel Bensson at Foods From Sweden
Renzo Bentsik at Foodhouse
Angela Boggiano who cooked some of the recipes and was a good laff
Eric Brazer master lobster fisherman
Alastair Brown and Jane Cumberbatch of Sierra Rica, Aracena
Simon Brown for encouraging me to take snaps
Pierre Bruno of Isigny Saint-Mère
Bulent at Alternative Travel
Simon Burgess and Susie Fairfax at Axis

**C**
Chantal Coady, chocolatier par excellence
Ilse Crawford for friendship, encouragement and inspiration

**D**
Hacer Develi
Francoise Dietrich who designed this book
Tom Dixon

**E**
Lewis Esson, my unfailingly charming, infallible editor
Mary Evans for guiding and trusting me!

**F**
Michele Franzolin the passionate chef at Al Duca
Anne Furniss, she of the clear, strong vision

**G**
Frances Gould, Theo, Phoebe and Tommy: Love, pure tearful happy Love
Simon Gould, Honey, Arron and Angel: my family, who are also my best friends
Mark Gould, Pam, Ethan and Daisy: far away, but still close
Marlene and David Gould: whom I love to honour
Chip Gray, The Harraseeket Inn, Freeport, Maine

**I**
Icelandair: great food in first class!
IKEA of Sweden: especially Catrin Termen and Roland Norberg

**J**
Joe's Basement

**L**
Le Creuset: strong, practical cast cookware, spatulas and Sabatier knives
Leica Cameras
Jason Lowe for encouraging me to take snaps

**M**
Dawn Mackin, common sense, sound judgement and an excellent cook
Eddie Mackin, an asset to be appreciated: so smart and steadfast
Joel Meslin, a magician in the kitchen
Metro Imaging
Hazrettin Mevlana
Jane Milton, who cooked some of the recipes and procured friends
All at Mohsen Restaurant

**N**
Vicdan, Eren and Emir Nil, my friends and guardians of Gûven's flame
Bert and Geraldine Nisonoff, for convivial companionship

**O**
Jane O'Shea, so smart and so focussed

**P**
Oscar Peña– who really knows how to love and live life with abandon

**Q**
All the people who put in so much hard work at Quadrille

**R**
Bill and Charlotte Reynolds – Swaddles Green Farm
Anna Maria Rossi, and Fabio, too
Machiko and Max Rutherston, who bridge London and Tokyo

**S**
John Scott and Berrin Torolsan, publishers of ever-excellent Cornucopia
Singapore Tourist Office
Ted Spitzer at Portland Public Market, Maine
David Stewart, Wyborowka Vodka
Minoo Sueke, for memorable meals
Jane Suthering for her invaluable experience, energy and sensitivity
Nicki Symington, for the opportunity to learn more

**T**
All at Tasting Australia and the City of Adelaide

**V**
Carlos Vargas, a gypsy who makes food sing

**W**
Westminster Hotel, Paris for the comfortable room and the full tummy

## bibliography

In writing this book, I have borrowed from, or been influenced by the following:

Coleman Barks
*Delicious Laughter, versions of Rumi*, Maypop Books, Athens 1990

J. G. Bennett
*Witness*, Bennet Books, 1989

Shaykh Moinuddin Chisti
*The Book of Sufi Healing*
Inner Traditions, Vermont 1991

Linda Collister and Anthony Blake, *The Bread Book*
Conran Octopus, London 1993

His Holiness the Dalai Lama
*A Flash of Lightning in a Dark Night*, Shambala Publications, Boston, Mass. 1998
*Freedom in Exile,* Hodder and Stoughton, London 1997

John Edwards
*The Roman Cookery of Apicius*
Random House/Century, London 1984

Reshad Feild, *The Last Barrier*
Element Books, Shaftesbury, 1981
*Breathing Alive*
Element Books, Shaftesbury, 1985

*Poems of Arab Andalucia*
trans. Cole Franzen, City Lights Books, San Francisco 1989

Khalil Gibran
*The Prophet*
William Heinemann, London 1974

Jane Grigson
*The Fruit Book*
Penguin, London 1978

Hallgarten and Cordell
*Reminiscences and Recipes of the Bukharan Jews of Samaqand* (booklet)
Jewish Museum, London 2000

Marcella Hazan
*Second Classic Italian Cookbook*
Papermac, London 1983

B. K. Iyengar
*Light on Yoga*
Thorsons, London 1966

J. Krishnamurti
*Collected works of J. Krishnamurti*
Kendal/Hunt Publishing, Dubuque 1977

Leif Männerstrøm
*Leif Männerstrøm*
Page One Publishing, Stockholm 1996

Julianne Margelashvili
*The Classic Cuisine of Soviet Georgia*
Prentice Hall Press, Columbus, New York 1991

Alan Moorhead
*Gallipoli*
Wordsworth Editions, 1998

P. D. Ouspensky
*In Search of the Miraculous*
Harvest Books, 1994

Claudia Roden
*A New Book of Middle Eastern Cuisine*
Penguin, London 1968
*The Food of Italy*
Chatto and Windus / Vintage, London 1999

Jeladda'din bin Rumi
*The Mathnawi / The Diwan of Shams-I-Tabrizi / Fihi ma Fihi*
trans. RA Nicholson
Octagon Press / Gibb Memorial Trust, 1979

*The Gourmet Quotation Book*
ed. Jennifer Taylor
Robert Hale, London 1995

Neale David Walsch
*Conversations With God, Part 1*
Putnam Publishing, 1996

Various
*The Swedish Kitchen*
Bokfrolog, Stockholm 1984

## index